AROUND
THE WORLD IN
EIGHTY-ONE
YEARS

AROUND THE WORLD IN EIGHTY-ONE YEARS

ROBERT MORLEY

A John Curtis Book
Hodder & Stoughton
LONDON SYDNEY AUCKLAND TORONTO

British Library Cataloguing in Publication Data

Morley, Robert, *1908–*
   Around the world in eighty-one years.
   1. Journeys round the world
   I. Title
   910.41

ISBN 0-340-53483 4

Published by Hodder and Stoughton,
a division of Hodder and Stoughton Ltd,
Mill Road, Dunton Green, Sevenoaks, Kent TN13 2YA
Editorial Office: 47 Bedford Square, London WC1B 3DP

Photoset by Litho Link Ltd., Welshpool, Powys, Wales

Printed in Great Britain by Butler and Tanner Ltd, Frome and London

CONTENTS

*Dedicated to anyone who
ever bought me a ticket*

Introduction

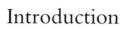

The camera is in position and so am I

INTRODUCTION

EVERY TIME the camera is ready to turn with all the lamps lit, the sound recorder alerted, the boom swinger precariously positioned on his step ladder, the most junior member of the crew makes his request:

"If we could see you once on your mark, Mr Morley." And I take up my stance toeing the chalk line or the batten nailed to the studio floor and face the camera while he unfurls his tape and measures the distance to the exact tip of my nose and makes a final adjustment of the focus. Life presents no problems. A swift glance floorwards and all is in order. But, once the camera is turning you mustn't, of course, look down. Even supposing you know what to say, have planned the appropriate expression you intend to adopt, however mellifluous your delivery – all is often in vain.

"Cut," cries the director, taking his cue from the hopeless shrug of the lighting expert. "I'm afraid", he says, "you failed to hit your mark."

Six inches – how can it matter? Alas, it does.

In the theatre or, indeed, in life there are no such interruptions. You may say that is a pity, but I can't agree. In life nothing is ever abandoned on the cutting-room floor. No foot of film remains undeveloped. Life is not an exact science and more often than not you have missed your mark. Some manage better than most, but, for myself, most times I have been wide of the mark often as a result of the clumsiness that has been largely my own from earliest times, when I impaled myself on the nursery key, to the present, when I struggle to insert a new battery in the hearing aid. Clumsiness is by no means to be despised. Others may deride, but are secretly proud of being unable to mend fuses, of never catching the ball, of failing to tie up parcels. Clumsiness, we tell ourselves, is a blessing reserved for those who think.

"Don't expect me to be able to manage a punt," an old friend confided, "I am in essence a theatrical director." And over we went.

Invited once to contribute an autobiographical note, I was tempted to append "destined for the diplomatic service," a claim as absurd as any I have made. Yet it stuck, and I am still occasionally asked why I never became an ambassador.

"It was Father's idea," I tell them.

After a conspicuously unsuccessful childhood, destiny still gave no hint of what I was to become until I found myself selling vacuum cleaners on the doorsteps of suburbia or, to be accurate, not selling vacuum cleaners. On the road to Kingston-on-Thames came the revelation: "You are never going to manage to sell anything but yourself." And so it proved. If you are not born to find your mark, better make your own. Happier to be a bull in a china shop than a cultural attaché. But how did the bull get into the china shop? Was he being driven to the slaughter house and somehow managed to elude the drover? Was it a last desperate attempt to avoid destruction?

"It came to pieces in my hands, Madam," – the stock excuse of the Parlourmaid. Our first parlourmaid, who was also my nurse, was cleaning the silver when she suddenly observed that her other charge was turning blue and saved my life with a slurp of brandy. Her good deed accomplished, she emigrated to Detroit. I made a pilgrimage of thanksgiving many years later. It should have proved an emotional reunion, but alas she had forgotten the entire incident.

"You saved my life, Nannie Gilbert," I told her.

"If you say so, Master Robert. But where on earth did I find the brandy, do you suppose?"

"In the medicine cupboard," I hazarded.

"That must have been it," she sounded relieved. "You were

always one to solve puzzles."

"But I was only four when you left me," I told her.

"Very sharp for your age even in those days and look at you now," she affirmed.

Very sharp indeed. So what then do I think of the world over which I have travelled all this time? It sounds ungrateful to confess it, but I still haven't the slightest idea of what it is all about. Does it have a purpose or even a use? For that matter, do I? Is it, as some imagine, a pleasant (or not so pleasant) stop-over on the road to eternity? Ought one to spend the time on Earth preparing for something else – and if so what?

I was once advised by an eminent guru crouched in a bungalow in Delhi not to bother my head about such things. I don't think I ever did. Curiosity, as mother taught, killed the cat. It is extraordinary how perfectly idiotic phrases still circulate through my head. Why, at least once during the day, do I repeat (sometimes aloud) a refrain heard originally listening to the Western Brothers?

> *"Which do you like the best?*
> *The plain or the hairy chest?*
> *Or perhaps, like Radcliffe Hall,*
> *You don't care for men at all."*

What am I to Ms Hall or she to me for that matter? Why am I a compulsive counter of paces before I find myself sitting in a particular location? Why do I recall the cut-out pointers marching beside the railway track? Why am I unable to forget that "the Pickwick, the Owl and the Waverley Pen come as a boon and a blessing to men"?

I dread to banish the rubbish of memory lest age should complete the process and one can no longer remember if one has had one's afternoon tea. I strive to remember the seven wonders of the world, which serves to remind me that I never saw the Hanging Gardens or the Tower of Babylon. My own wonders were even more absurd – my first railway ticket to Weymouth, the script of my first play so beautifully typed in blue by Ethel Christian, the blind and deaf Miss Keller, who communicated with finger taps, and Greta Garbo, who told me how lucky I was to be able to drive a car and go to Australia. I did manage to see the other sphinx, but I am not even sure it was included in the original list.

Unlike the fictitious Fogg who managed to circle the globe in days, my adventure round the world has been a frequently interrupted feast – more like a series of visits to an elaborate buffet rather than a place at a banquet table. It has, however, been no less tasty.

As this book demonstrates I hopscotched rather than trekked and never stayed long away from base camp.

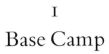

I

Base Camp

Let's start at the beginning

I

BASE CAMP

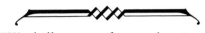

"We shall not cease from exploration
And the end of our exploring
Will be to arrive where we started
And know that place for the first time."

T. S. ELIOT

I ALWAYS INTEND to go back to Folkestone, where I spent a great deal of my childhood. In Saxon times it was called 'Fulchanstane' – literally, the rock on which the folk gathered. And what became of the folk of my childhood? How are the Boddam-Whettams, the Gees, the Mackesons, the Forbes? All dead, I fear.

As a child I was afraid of dogs, of course, and also bitterly resented being sent on errands. Yet I seem to have spent a lifetime doing just that – dispatched hither and thither with an air ticket and a film contract.

We lived all over the place in Folkestone: Augusta Gardens, Earl's Avenue, Bouverie Road, West Radnor Gardens – and even on the Leas itself. The Leas were the Royal Enclosure of Folkestone – a vast expanse of lawns and flower gardens perched on the clifftop with pines and broom tumbling, Riviera-style, down to the promenades on sea level. On the Leas was a statue of Folkestone's greatest son, William Harvey, the discoverer of the circulation of the blood, who was born there in 1578. He stands holding his heart in his hand. Thousands of medical men got together to pay for that statue and Folkestone is proud of it, and of him.

At one end of the Leas stood two enormous hotels, the Grand and the Metropole. Between them a lift ran down the cliff to the ocean below; it cost a penny to ride. Our nurse made us walk down, but, coming up, my sister and I sat expectant on wooden seats, waiting for the deafening hydraulic splash which marked the beginning of the ascent. Halfway up – exactly halfway – we passed our twin descending.

On rough days at the bottom, Nanny would take us to the harbour. Seasick passengers in a woebegone huddle left the ferries and boarded waiting trains.

"That's what comes of going abroad, Master Robert," she would tell me.

On fine Sundays, after church, the bands played. There were two bands and two bandstands. The deckchairs and the bathchairs came out, the latter with two attendants – one to pull and the other to push. Folkestone lived it up in those days.

On the hilltop near the end of the Leas stands the Church of St Mary and St Eanswythe. St Eanswythe, the patron saint of Folkestone, was the grand-daughter of the Kentish King Ethelbert, who was converted by St Augustine – he who called us not Angles but Angels. She founded a nunnery in 630, most say on the spot where the church now stands. Rather peculiar miracles are attributed to the lady. There was the time when, while building her nunnery, a carpenter sawed a roof beam three feet too short. Wood must have been at a premium because, instead of ordering up another piece, she merely prayed and extended the timber to the required length. Or perhaps it was a case of waste not want not. She also forbade ravenous birds to gather in Folkestone and, it is said, they obeyed.

But Church for us meant Holy Trinity and that meant the Rev. W. H. Elliot, later to become Canon Elliot, later to preach to the King, to become the radio parson, to have a weekly column in the *Daily Sketch*, to become quite mad and to be visited by me in a vast mental hospital.

"Bring me detective stories," he would urge me, "and get me out."

I'm not sure he really wanted out – he had suddenly lost his faith and there was nowhere to go. But in the days of my youth at Folkestone people crowded into his church an hour before the service was due to start to be sure of a place to hear him preach.

A more secular diversion was Folkestone Central Railway Station. The platforms were built extravagantly tall and approached by a very steep incline. Once launched on the way down, it was all but impossible to stop. My sister and I sped on, aware that at the bottom we might just possibly be killed by a passing bus. It had happened once, or so we were told, so why not again? Not that we wanted to die. We were all too fond of Folkestone. But why were we, I sometimes ask myself. What was it about the place that ensured my everlasting affection? Why does it still capture my undivided attention when I read of some incident involving the town?

"WOMAN KNOCKED DOWN BY BUS IN FOLKESTONE
 HIGH STREET"
"FERRY SERVICE SUSPENDED IN CHANNEL PORT"
"FAMOUS KENT LANDMARK SUGAR LOAF FACES
 SUBSIDENCE"
"SHORNCLIFFE CAMPS LIKELY REFUGE FOR HONG KONG
 BOAT PEOPLE"

Now, just three miles north-east of the centre of the town, land has been earmarked as the site of the British terminal of the Channel tunnel. Things are always happening in Folkestone. But then they always were.

There were the croquet tournaments in the Pleasure Gardens. There was the Pleasure Garden Theatre itself with Clarkson Rose and once even Oscar Ashe in pantomime. Esmé Percy performed in *The Doctor's Dilemma* there and so impressed me that I was obliged to become an actor myself. Besides the theatre, there were three cinemas changing programmes twice weekly. The hours Mother and I spent in the dark – she in love with Clive Brook and myself (when old enough) in love with Lillian Harvey!

There was Mr Webb, who popped a chocolate finger into my mouth as soon as I appeared in his grocery shop. Can you imagine that happening these days in Waitrose?

There was waiting in the hall of the Radnor Club for father to finish his rubber of bridge and on the way home sometimes there was a meringue at Geronimo's.

There was roller-skating near the pier and the pier itself – and the slots! A penny in the slot and the little boat emerged which had to be steered between the rocks and into the harbour if you wanted your penny returned. There was the hangman who supervised the execution of the miscreant and the prison gates which closed on a dangling corpse. There was no chance there of getting your penny back, but it had been well spent. There was the slot that took your penny and showed you a fireman rescuing a maiden and Sweeney Todd cutting a throat or two before dispatching the bodies down a chute, and the cranes which somehow always dropped the penny bars just when you were certain that this time you had been lucky.

Still, you were sure to be lucky on the shingle beneath the pier, where a man trudged with an enormous basket loaded with barley sugar and currant buns, paper windmills, bottles of fizz (not vulgar champagne, but raspberry cordial) sealed with a glass marble entrapped by wire and not at all easy to prise open.

This was the beach where I once dug down determined to reach Australia, which some idiot had told me lay beneath. Indeed the texture had begun to change, moisture to seep in and then, at the moment of anticipated triumph, I was captured for tea. Not captured perhaps – I was a willing prisoner to food.

But what was it about Folkestone that captured me then and has ever since held me in thrall? Others, no doubt, feel the same about Budleigh Salterton, Brighton or Inverness. The point surely is that this is the place where my sister and I came to terms with ourselves, learned who we were and, realizing we were stuck with ourselves, vowed to make the best of it. We settled for second best, or third or even fourth. We were never to be top of the class or the most popular children in the world. We were never to be picked for the team. My constant companion was to be myself with all the advantages and disadvantages that entailed. My sister and I had a secret language: each called the other 'Yub'. It never seemed worthwhile to understand, still less to listen, to other tongues. In Folkestone I at least learned to be self-sufficient – to aim to please the one person with whom I was stuck, myself. My sister did the same. I cherished her reputed comment on seeing the ocean, or at least being aware of its purpose:

"A great big bath for Margaret Morley."

In later years things were different. She seldom bothered to sail away, except for one stifled excursion to South Africa in search, I suppose, of a husband. Eventually she made a fairly disastrous marriage with an eccentric member of the Guards. Margaret spent most of her life in Kent, never straying all that far from Folkestone, while I ventured further afield. I suppose we still loved each other in a way, but, whenever we met, we seemed to argue. The doctor who tended her when she was dying told me she was the bravest patient he had ever known. I used to sit by her bedside and argue about Thatcher. We had better things to talk about, but I was the one who persisted. I was not a natural talk-show guest. I barely let anyone finish their stories before I was off on one of my own. A child who for years clung to the belief that there were real circuses in Piccadilly and Holborn learned in Folkestone to become his own clown – and even ringmaster.

"There is nothing on earth intended for innocent people so horrible as a school. To begin with, it is a prison. But it is in some respects more cruel than a prison. In a prison, for instance, you are not forced to read books written by the warders and the governor."

G. B. SHAW

Nothing prepared me for Wellington College, not even the fact that in earlier childhood the family had once rented a house called Underwood in the grounds. There, during the First World War, Mother and Father hoarded Tiptree jams in the loft. They shared a passion for the confections and dreaded a lack of them.

The buildings of Wellington College itself were as forbidding to me as those of the nearby establishment for the criminally insane, Broadmoor. Over an archway leading to the Master's house was engraved: "Not once or twice in this our island's story the path of duty was the way to glory."

The Master himself was called Malim and wore a double-breasted suit with an extravagantly long jacket. I spoke to him once and only once – on the day I was to leave, after serving two or possibly three years of my term. It was not only an unexpected release it was also, with fortuitous timing, before the exams were about to start.

"You are the boy who is going home," he said, looking up from a report compiled by my housemaster, and added, "goodbye then."

I never discovered the reason for my welcome release. During the ensuing holiday a doctor gave his opinion: "If you send him back," he told my parents, "he might die."

Were things really that bad? I like to think so, naturally. My daughter-in-law questioned some of my contemporaries years afterwards.

"Quite a jolly child", they told her, "with a fatal habit of answering back."

I myself had my revenge in a BBC documentary when I knelt on a chair and demonstrated how I was beaten by prefects for slacking at cricket. Not that I merely slacked: I waited for my chance to bat and then knocked down the stumps. It was a protest that led to the inevitable swishing in the bathroom, which provided a space for my tormentors to take a running swipe.

I suppose, if Wellington taught me anything, it was never to make the best of things. In the end I was excused cricket and sentenced to the shooting range. I seldom hit a target. I never learned to look through my right eye. The first time I took to glasses in middle age the optician diagnosed what he called a lazy eye.

"You have had it all your life," he told me.

"It is monstrous", I said, "that they never discovered it at Wellington."

"You were lucky they didn't. You would have had to wear glasses that much sooner. Mind you, if the other eye goes, this one will come into service. What surprises me is that you never tried shooting off the other shoulder."

"Because", I told him, "I can't close my eyes separately."

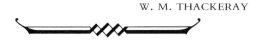

"Torture in a public school is as much licensed as the knout in Russia."

W. M. THACKERAY

I suppose the real reason I was so unhappy at Wellington had nothing to do with a lazy eye. I suppose I was the wrong shape, a deeply unattractive boy, never able to make friends or even lovers. The prefect's pet – or for that matter the Beak's – was not to be my role. The latter were a very rum lot. What happened to them all, I sometimes wonder. One of them at least served time later for gross indecency. He almost beat indiscriminately – but not quite. He slippered the chosen across his knees.

I lived at Wellesley House, marginally more civilized than the dormitories, but it was such a distance from the main buildings that one was kept on the run.

My housemaster composed long sentences: "I must not in future pick my nose in class; I must use a handkerchief and never pause to admire the result, but fold it back neatly in my pocket." Then he would command, "Write that out 500 times and bring it to me before lock-up tomorrow."

It was a fairly impossible task. If you went to him later to plead, he would reduce the number to more manageable proportions. His son-in-law taught maths and batted the tassel of the window blind without pausing for the whole period. All the staff were in need of psychiatric treatment and a good many of the boys too before they had finished with them.

Mr Tallboys, who taught English, never bothered to learn our names.

"The fat boy on the end. Amuse me," he would urge. One rose and did one's best, but he was seldom satisfied. He read

Saki out loud to us and a story about a gnat who flew into the nostril of a Roman Emperor and grew into an eagle with claws of brass and a beak of gold. I have never found that tale in any book. Perhaps he had written it himself.

Some masters were more ghastly than others, but only one (who was elaborately perfumed and never rose in the morning for early pre-breakfast classes) actually paid cash for good essays. I suppose that is why I became a journalist. One needed cash for the tuck shop, where they dished out ice cream and even strawberries in season.

Wellington was, of course, a military college founded in 1853 mainly for the sons of deceased army officers. So there was compulsory Officers' Training Corps. The first time I was faced with that I was set the task of donning puttees, the strip of cloth which you had to wind around your leg from ankle to knee. I wound them upside down and was given six extra parades. Not that they helped.

Once a year we were examined by real soldiers from nearby Aldershot, giving us a chance to rise from the ranks.

"Move to the right in columns of four," they would bark – such useless instructions. I preferred to march straight ahead through the goalposts and off the field. Naturally I failed to become even a corporal.

I loathed everything – even the surrounding acres of dry bracken, which I decided to incinerate. The conflagration burned for hours. My companion and I were urged to own up in lieu of cancelled half-holidays for the whole school. I never did and everybody sweated it out for three Wednesdays. It was much better for them, I told myself, than wasting time playing Rugby. They'd only have got scrum pox. Everyone at Wellington caught the nasty skin eruption sooner or later. It necessitated yellow paint on one's countenance.

I was never happy in Crowthorne. Well, maybe just the once as alone on a Berkshire railway station I waited for the train to take me away.

"A man should know something of his own country, too, before he goes abroad."

LAURENCE STERNE

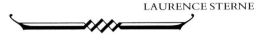

Both sets of grandparents lived on opposite sides of the same square – gardens actually: Courtfield Gardens, South Kensington. We never ventured north of Hyde Park except when one of our grandmothers took us shopping in Oxford Street to Selfridge's chocolate department. The store packaged their chocolates in white boxes with a paper frill round the edge. When the sweets ran out, there was one final treat: if you tore off the frill, the noise produced was exactly as if one had fired a Maxim gun. Never having experienced machine-gun fire at first hand, it was our favourite sound.

Grandmother and Lady Gorringe (whose husband owned another once famous department store) shared a brougham. When the latter was dying, they covered the roadway with straw. They only did that for ladies or, I suppose, gentlemen of title. It was the ultimate status symbol, but they died nevertheless. It was a long time ago. If you shopped from a carriage at the original Harrods, Mr Burbage, the proprietor, used to emerge from the store in a boater to take the fish order. He was primarily a fishmonger and poulterer. Later he built on the other side of Brompton Road the most famous department store in the world. He also built a beautiful mansion in Pinewood, Buckinghamshire. Later, much later, after it had become a film studio, I was to sleep in his bedroom – possibly even his bed – when I was filming Gilbert in *Gilbert and Sullivan*.

"No one could ever be certain of the afterlife or the exact end of the Cromwell Road."

OSCAR WILDE

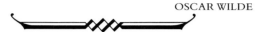

Round and about, the neighbourhood has changed surprisingly little over the years. In bad times Mother and Father would retreat to one of the various small private hotels in the area, embarrassed (at least Mother was) by the lack of small change with which to tip the staff. Father kept us short of cash. Father kept himself short of cash also for that matter. On Sundays he took me to inspect the horse flesh at Tattersalls on Knightsbridge Green. As a cavalry officer, he would sometimes venture into the loose boxes and emit an odd chuckling sound, which indicated to the occupant his wish for the brute to shift his hind quarters. Sometimes he would give instructions to one of the handlers to parade the steed and trot along the cobblestones. The fellow obviously expected a tip, but my parent indicated he would see him in the morning and include it in the purchase price. In the sale catalogue the name of the vendor was always disguised by a soubriquet: 'the Property of a Gentleman'. The reason given for selling the animal was always to 'dissolve a partnership'. What, I wondered, would Father do with a horse? Tie him to the lamppost outside the Naval and Military Hotel? In the hall I still have a drawing of him driving a coach and four round Hyde Park.

"It is my belief, Watson, founded on my experience, that the lowest and vilest alleys of London do not present a more dreadful record of sin than does the smiling and beautiful countryside."

SHERLOCK HOLMES

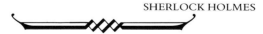

When I was not cringing in a horsebox, Father and I sometimes took bus rides around London. Once, disembarking, he took me for a stroll in Jermyn Street.

"There are men in this street," he informed me, "who paint their faces."

Once more I cowered fearful of Red Indian arrows. Although too shy to inform me of sexual perversion, he thought it part of my education to apprise me of the danger of drugs. We journeyed on a bus to Limehouse, where Father entered what he imagined to be an opium den masquerading as a small Chinese grocery shop.

"Got any snow, mother?" he asked the elderly custodian.

"You want to come in winter," she told him.

He retired baffled. "A very secretive lot the Chinese," he remarked.

After my father gave up his dream that I would master a foreign tongue and almost immediately become an ambassador, I got a job selling lager beer. I was summarily dismissed when a customer swallowed a draught of sea water drawn from a cask I had had delivered to the Café Royal. Careless of him, I always thought, but there was no doubt in my mind that the cask has been broached by the wicked sailors who had transported it from Czechoslovakia. I was unjustly held responsible, although I hadn't even been on board at the time.

It was soon realized by the family that I was unlikely to earn an honest living and I was allowed to try the stage. My mother, who had hitherto been known as 'poor Daisy' because of her disastrous marriage, now become 'poor, poor Daisy'. To have a disastrous husband was one thing, but to have a disastrous son was simply too much.

I spent a year at the Academy of Dramatic Art in Gower Street behind the British Museum. There was a final meeting with the principal.

"Tell me, Morley," he enquired, "do you have private means?"

Taking the implied caution, I left to become a 'responsible gentleman', which was the trade description of a small-part actor specializing in playing solicitors – or, at a pinch, coroners.

Twice a week we made the rounds of Leicester Square and the offices of agents. "Nothing this morning," we were usually informed after knocking at the doors and small windows above us having been opened in order to identify the supplicant. Occasionally we struck lucky and were dispatched on a forty-week tour of *The Private Secretary* or *Charley's Aunt*.

"The part carries £4 0s. 0d," we were informed. It was useless to try for £4 10s. 0d.

Sometimes the tour would founder. Once, stranded in Reading, I sought out the resident manager of the theatre.

"I shall have to walk back to London if I don't get this week's money," I told him.

"Well, what do you expect me to do? Walk with you? You'd better get started," was the brusque reply.

The dates we were expected to fill, if all went well, were printed on small pink cards like dance programmes, but with no pencil attached. Old actors would grumble if, months ahead, a week were still left blank. There was a certain security about the work and I learned in time my first lesson: play the audience and not the part. It was a happy life for ten years. I managed to increase my salary from £4 0s. 0d to £8 0s. 0d.

Then came a lucky break. I was cast as Oscar Wilde – an irresponsible gentleman if there ever was one – at the Gate Theatre on Villiers Street in London. Mysteriously, I became a leading man. There were a few hiccups along the way, but eventually I arrived on Shaftesbury Avenue – Theatreland.

"Whereas . . . the distracted state of England . . .
call[s] for all possible means to appease and avert the
wrath of God . . . it is thought fit and ordered by the
Lords and Commons in this Parliament assembled, that
. . . public stage-plays shall cease and be forborne."
ORDINANCE OF PARLIAMENT, 2 Sept. 1642

Theatreland has always been for me that little nest of adjacent properties in Shaftesbury Avenue . . . the Lyric, the Globe, the Apollo, and the Queen's.

How I loved showing off. When the casinos opened near by, I even learned to look forward to matinées. The curtain came down, I made a brief stop at the box-office to secure the current advance and then went off behind the Lyric Theatre to Archer Street and the Golden Nugget or possibly the Golden Horseshoe or Charlie Chester's to the green baize roulette wheel and the occasional glimpse of painter Francis Bacon.

Sometimes, while waiting for the coffers to fill, I learned the secrets of the box-office.

"Why did you only offer an upper-circle ticket", I would demand, "with all those stalls to fill – let alone the boxes?"

"Leave it to me," was the reply. "I've spent twenty years sizing up the paying public."

In those days we were in the hands of the agencies and not the touts. The head of Ashton Mitchell did the deal usually after the first act. If he didn't guarantee the run for six months you were in trouble. Nowadays you need a small hired queue under the sign RETURN TICKETS to advertise your wares and tempt the tourists. They also sell who only stand and wait.

"It hath evermore been the notorious badge of prostituted Strumpets and the lewdest Harlots, to ramble abroad to plays, to Playhouses; whither no honest, chaste or sober Girls or Women but only branded Whores and infamous Adulteresses did usually resort in ancient times."

WILLIAM PRYNNE

The Lyric was always my luckiest theatre. For one thing the stage door was in Great Windmill Street, the liveliest street in Soho. The salt beef sandwiches and discreet post-cards pinned to the doorposts: 'Tall Model, please walk up', 'Strict Disciplinarian – appointments only' . . . the cowboy taxi offices . . . the courtyard where the fruit barrows unloaded . . . the wonderful little Piccadilly Bistro . . . the beggars . . . the buggers . . . the pimps. There was the game of Find the Lady, which occasionally allowed me to win a few fivers, which were speedily claimed back by the minders, and at the top of the street there was that mysterious Glove Shop.

Once, during the war, making a film under the direction of Jack Raymond, I professed to take a cheerful view of the fall of Paris.

He looked puzzled and woebegone. "Paris", he told me, "was the last city in the world where you could get kid gloves up to the armpits." He indicated the length and for a moment I wondered if he was a transvestite.

"Surely not," I comforted. "There is always Great Windmill Street – right at the top on the left."

"You mean Archer Street," he retorted, "and as usual you don't know what you're talking about."

But, to return to the stage door of the Lyric, as I so often did, and right next door to the Windmill Theatre, which boasted a magnificent canteen where I took tea with Tommy Steele and his girl friends. There was, of course, nothing similar behind the scenes of the Lyric. Once past the doorkeeper, you were in the world of bleak austerity. Actors sometimes made the best of their dressing-rooms, but not before the first night was safely past and they were assured of a few weeks before the closure notice went up. Cushions, coloured tablecloths, photographs of loved ones, telegrams of good wishes pinned to the mirror, a space cleared for the gin bottle and, if you were Ralph Richardson, sometimes a pet rat scampering around. Myself, I preferred the austere, the sense of impermanence – except of course for the gin. The tax inspector once accused me of serving all callers and not just those who came strictly on business. I pointed out that I could not be expected to search and discover a contract lurking in their pocket as they came through the door.

Next-door-but-one to the Lyric was the Queen's, where I had my first play produced with an all star cast: Marie Tempest, Sybil Thorndike, Margaret Rutherford and Rex Harrison. It was a poor little thing, but mine own. It didn't run long, nor did it deserve to, but it was then that I first met Hugh ('Binkie') Beaumont, who presented it on behalf of H. M. Tennent, then and for a long time the most successful management in London. In a sense Tennent's were the only management. There were, of course, others – Bronson Albery, Henry Sherek, Firth Shepherd, but, whereas Albery was the traditionalist, Firth the vulgarian who slept with his leading ladies and sometimes married them, Sherek prodigious of appetite and girth – Binkie Beaumont was the Grand Master of the Game. He plotted and moved his pieces on the board, sometimes had as many as five or six plays running in the West End and, most importantly, spoke every language but his own. To Binkie, actors were clients and not employees. They were children to be played with, philosophers with whom to discuss scripts, beautiful women to be made to look even lovelier in the hands of top couturiers. And there were those actors, like myself, who wanted everything made easy. He kept his word. He told his clients what they wanted to hear even if, sometimes, they hadn't listened carefully enough and only heard what they wanted. Everything about him was immaculate, with the exception of the smallest and most intimidating elevator in London which bore you aloft to his office. In the days when all the other homosexuals were simply queer, he was the original gay member of the tribe. His equanimity was imperturbable. Triumphs and disasters were both impostors to him. I did half a dozen plays under his banner, which he unfurled only in battle and round which we rallied. His arrival on the scene was as sudden and mysterious as his departure, but far less tragic. A knight in shining armour is too fanciful an obituary, but he fought our battles for us and kept his armour polished almost to the end.

For thirty or forty years the magic and mystery of Soho and theatreland persisted and then evaporated. Nowadays I can't bear London. Dirty, overcrowded, traffic blocked. Has the city changed or have I? Both, of course. I am perpetually waiting for the lights to change, yet, when they do, still nothing moves. Frustration poisons the air far more than petrol fumes. Everyone is late for something or other. No one has allowed enough time or expected a fire in Wigmore Street. The entire population is in a hurry, although it is already too late. Worst of all are the couriers on motorcycles who still press on to be collected by ambulances to fill the casualty wards. There is the ludicrous folly of advertisements: how to save money by spending it; above all, those that urge you to keep moving by train, by bus, by plane. You sit and stare at them realizing that moving is the one thing you are unlikely to do.

"Oxford is on the whole more attractive than Cambridge to the ordinary visitor; and the traveller is therefore recommended to visit Cambridge first, or to omit it altogether if he cannot visit both."

BAEDEKER'S *Great Britain*, 1887

The first time I saw Sir John Martin Harvey he was reciting "Boots" at a charity matinée. In the tradition of an actor-manager of his day he declaimed the piece. I was surprised at how small he was. Seldom deigning to appear in the West End, he spent most years touring in *The Burgomaster of Steelmonde*. It was an inexplicable choice – except for the box-office receipts. I think he also followed Henry Irving in *The Bells*. His leading lady was his wife, billed as Miss N. de Silva and an appallingly bad actress. Without her, critics averred, he would have been the leading actor of his day. Presently he bought a first play from a friend of mine. He was always going to appear in it, but never did.

On one of my rare visits to his home I noted that Miss de Silva always referred to him as "G.M." Puzzled I enquired of my friend the meaning of this soubriquet.

"G.M.", he explained, "stands for Great Man."

Harvey once asked if I had been up at Cambridge.

I lied.

"Which college?" he probed.

"Keble," I replied hoping there was one. It seems there is, but it is at Oxford – Harvey, however, didn't seem to notice.

"I suppose", he went on, "you never visited that preposterous Festival Theatre."

"I don't think so," I lied again.

G.M. expressed satisfaction. A peacock shrilled – at least I'm pretty sure it wasn't a cock crowing.

Was the Festival Theatre at which I spent a very happy

season as preposterous as all that? Some thought Terence Grey, who owned it, was a genius ahead of his time. He installed the most advanced lighting of the period – a solid cyclorama lit by a multitude of spotlights. And he certainly didn't site the spots in the boxes. Such wanton extravagance in cutting down the seating capacity of the auditorium infuriates me every time I see it. Come to think of it, I don't remember there being any boxes at the Festival Theatre, but there were many innovations. The programmes could be read in the auditorium if one held the centrefold open and tilted it towards the stage. Every member of the audience tried this at least once, producing a continuous crackle throughout the performances.

Grey was a bearded giant with a most appalling stammer. His notes to the actors were never spoken, but always delivered typewritten by a secretary who was also his mistress. Legend had it that, once confronted with the infidelity of a former wife, he had broken down the bedroom door with an axe. He stood poised on the threshold, the guilty couple cowering on the marital couch. Then he discarded his weapon and stuck out his tongue.

He ran a sumptuous restaurant next door at an extravagant loss. But he had a curious ambivalence about money. He returned to his parents' mansion, Gog and Magog, for an afternoon and, while he was away, we confronted his manager with complaints about the lack of carpeting in our dressing-rooms. The manager had the whole establishment recarpeted in one afternoon. On his return, Terence's reaction was sharp and to the point. A note was sent immediately to the manager which read: "You have done it this time. You can bloody well pay for it and then you can bloody well get out." Yet Grey would never have considered sacking his chef, who every week prepared a duck pâté of such lingering taste and appalling smell that, while he was preparing his masterpiece, rehearsals had to be cancelled.

"For Cambridge people rarely smile
Being urban, squat and packed with guile."

RUPERT BROOKE

There was not a great deal of enthusiasm among the university students, nor indeed among the performers, when Grey presented a Latin comedy in which the cast was faced with masks constructed of absorbent rubber. They grew increasingly soggy with perspiration and saliva.

"What an extraordinary production," said an aunt of mine, who had wandered into a matinée. "You know the masks looked for all the world as if they were made of rubber. I don't believe the ancient Romans knew about that."

We gave the first performance of *1066 and All That* at the Festival Theatre and then proceeded to close the season, as far as Grey was concerned, with Wilde's *Salome*. But by that time we were all exhausted and, on my part at least, had only an imperfect knowledge of the role. Beatrix Lehmann joined the company as Salome and had had more time than the rest of us to study the script.

On the first night I skipped several pages and then realized, to my horror, that I was already offering her my peacocks and a coffer of nacre in an effort to persuade her not to demand the head of John the Baptist before she had even danced a step. The few undergraduates we had managed to persuade to attend were obviously going to be disappointed. Somehow I managed to retrace my path and the seven veils were eventually shed. Lehmann never forgave me. Terence never even noticed. He, as usual, was concerned that we had missed our spots. But then such things happen in repertory. What doesn't usually happen is one of the cast killing himself because of a bad notice in *Granta*; he should have read mine: "Robert Morley was trying in both senses of the word."

At the end of the season Mr Grey retired from the theatre

and became a wine grower in the South of France. It was a great loss to the theatre in general and to Cambridge in particular, but I hope he triumphed in the vineyards. He certainly deserved to do well.

"There was a rocky valley between Buxton and Bakewell . . . divine as the vale of Tempe; you might have seen the gods there morning and evening, Apollo and the sweet Muses of the Light . . . You enterprised a railroad, . . . you blasted its rocks away . . . And now, every fool in Buxton can be at Bakewell in half-an-hour, and every fool in Bakewell in Buxton."

JOHN RUSKIN

Before the war, each Sunday, bands of touring performers passed each other on the platforms of Crewe station. Wicker baskets full of costumes and props were shifted from one train to another. Touring meant trains, and trains meant changing direction at Crewe, which was the junction of the lines to Manchester, Liverpool, Birmingham and Chester.

If Sir Frank Benson were alive today, he would have been well over 130, but, when I toured under his banner, he was still approaching his seventieth birthday – he just seemed to be over a hundred. He was the original ancient mariner. Before the war people grew older far more rapidly than they have done since. Benson had weathered countless storms, given his first public performance with the Oxford University Dramatic Society playing the female role of Clytemnestra by Aeschylus in the original Greek. Indeed, he had even produced the piece way back in the 1880s. For many, many years he toured the provinces, directed proceedings at

Stratford and received the freedom of that city. He had been knighted by His Majesty the King on the occasion of performing *Julius Caesar* for the monarch celebrating Shakespeare's Tercentenary. His companies (and here I quote from *Who Was Who*) "were recognized as the nurseries of acting and many prominent London actors and actresses gained early experience under his management". I was one of them.

I first met 'Nannie' or 'Pa' as everyone called him in the sleazy confines of a Soho pub where he was rehearsing for yet another farewell tour. It was his custom when the curtain fell to embark on a farewell speech to the city in which he was appearing and in which he always claimed to have sold newspapers on the pavements. This was a surprising and quite fallacious admission. Benson had been educated at Winchester and New College, Oxford, and his attitude to the stage had always been not only ambivalent but also far removed from that of the conventional Shakespearian actor of his day. Members of his company were expected to pursue manly sports and were engaged as often as not for their prowess as spin bowlers or hockey centre-forwards as for their thespian skills. He believed that the ability 'to play the game' was the essential prerequisite of the strolling player and would do much to mitigate against the customary vulgarity of his chosen calling. This was, of course, in the good old days, which, at the time I met him, had already vanished as far as he was concerned. Separated from Lady Benson and as poor as the proverbial church mouse, his affairs were in the hands of H. V. Neilson, who kept him on short rations and long train journeys up and down the country in the company of a motley and hard-drinking crew, which numbered among the cast the only genuine hermaphrodite I ever encountered and who acted as the wardrobe person, and a leading lady who existed entirely on biscuits.

We played in whatever scenery the local theatre provided from stock carefully hoarded against the demands of the annual pantomime. We thought nothing of masking a deck-chair painted on the backcloth by remaining motionless in front of it in an attempt to add some sort of verisimilitude to the coast of Illyria.

There were eight different performances during the week and no expense incurred by a dress rehearsal. In the pit, the orchestra was hard pressed to pick up a cue and it was essential to apprise the conductor with a peremptory nod when the clown was about to break into song or when marvellous sweet music was the order of the day. Often the cue had to be delivered a number of times before the band actually struck up.

It was for Benson a sad end to what had been an illustrious career, but he kept his head high and his neck permanently encased in towelling and proceeded everywhere at a jog trot except at weekends when, whatever the distance, soberly and correctly clad he caught a night sleeper to London to attend a seance and spiritualist service in memory of a young actress on whose account he had deserted the marital nest and who had died soon after of tuberculosis.

Under Benson's tutelage I learnt first, when clasping a sword scabbard behind my back, not to stick out my bottom and, second, that an audience will seldom walk out en masse however dreadful the entertainment. Pa on the other hand never learned not to stay until the bitter end. Sometimes he would summon me to his dressing-room and attempt to improve my own performance with a half-remembered piece of business once long before invented by Oscar Ashe. On one occasion I reminded him that it was getting late and I still had to change my costume for the evening task and I hadn't as yet enjoyed my tea. He grasped my arm surprisingly vigorously and remarked that I had seen one side of him and now would witness another – but of course I never did.

During the trial scene in *The Merchant of Venice* he habitually forgot to provide himself with props. At some stage he would retire backward into the wings, where assistants would be waiting to thrust the scales, the dagger and the bond into his hands, held behind his back. Observing the manoeuvre, I enquired the purpose.

"When he walks backwards Pa believes he is invisible," I was told.

He delighted in entertaining in his dressing-room, during a performance, then, apprised of his cue about to be delivered, trotted on to the stage by the first available entrance. Often mistaking his role, he would bound forward to deliver a welcome from old Hardcastle dressed as Jacques. A courteous gentleman, members of his cast were always thanked later for having eventually got him back on course.

Old men forget, but I have never forgotten him. I have never forgotten his performances of Shylock, Jacques, Peter Teazle, Malvolio, Hardcastle in *She Stoops to Conquer* (something of a breather for him) and his surprising Caliban, in which he persisted in hanging upside down from a tree. His customary problem with his dentures was temporarily solved in this position. The one part Benson never played was King Lear – but then, of course, he lived it.

"What is this thing called health? Simply a state in which the individual happens transiently to be perfectly adapted to his environment. Obviously, such states cannot be common, for the environment is in constant flux."

H. L. MENCKEN

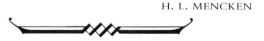

The chalybeate and salt springs of Leamington Spa attracted the attention of the health conscious as early as the eighteenth century. The first bath was opened there in 1786, but it really achieved fame when Queen Victoria, influenced by her physician, Dr Henry Jephson, awarded the town the prefix 'Royal'. It is now the last place in England where the waters can be taken under the NHS.

In the days when Leamington Spa boasted a theatre amongst its splendid Victorian and Regency buildings and its baths, it also figured as the home town of Watson Mill, who had written a hitherto unproduced play entitled *The Eternal Flame* and who met up with Russell Thorndike, in whose company I was appearing at the time on a prolonged tour of *Doctor Syn*, in which Russell played the smuggling parson of Romney Marsh. Russell, the tearaway brother of Sybil, was not only our bread and butter he was also (at least on his better evenings) a superb actor of the later Henry Irving school, from whom he had learned his craft. Sometimes he essayed Grand Guignol seasons in the West End with his distinguished and saintly sister, but more often crossed and recrossed the country settling in small provincial theatres with *Doctor Syn*. There were even the occasional full houses. But he was not the most reliable leading man even the provincial theatre possessed at the time. He occasionally absented himself from the proceedings and once was dis-covered in the nick of time queuing outside the doors of the local pit to watch his own performance. He was, however, generally in his dressing-room awaiting the arrival of his patrons and entertaining any nubile theatre usher who happened fortuitously to be available on the premises. Life was never dull with Russell, but we were hardly prepared for the excitement engendered when he announced that he was suspending the tour of *Doctor Syn* to stay on a fortnight in Leamington, where he proposed to appear in and present the world première of a new play, which the playwright himself was to finance and to which we were all invited.

At the first reading of the piece we discovered that Russell's role was that of a cat burglar caught in *flagrante delicto* in the mansion of his wealthy elder brother. It was, as far as he was concerned, in the nature of a grudge raid and it was revealed during the lengthy discussion following his arrest that their mother, not wanting a second child, had done her best (albeit unsuccessfully) to procure an abortion. This had physically impaired the health of the child and obliged him to scale the occasional drainpipe. The revelation seriously impeded the imminent marriage plans of the owner of the house, as his fiancée vigorously protested at her putative brother-in-law serving a prison sentence.

I cannot rightly explain her attitude, as Russell had cast a young lady for the part who had not previously appeared on any stage and, despite rigorous coaching, refused (or was unable) ever to speak except in a whisper. This was in the days before Equity and, indeed, before microphones.

I played a Duke with an immensely long cigarette holder and had one equally lengthy speech extolling the law of Karma, with which, until that moment, the audience and indeed myself had never been acquainted. However – and now we come to the reason that we had all followed our leader so loyally and with such great expectations – the last act mysteriously shifted to Westminster Abbey, where the Unknown Soldier was to emerge from his tomb and declare himself not only to be on the side of Mr Thorndike but also of universal peace. It was the first occasion that the Lord Chamberlain has permitted the depiction of the warrior and allowed him to comment adversely on the mud which appeared to be his main complaint against the folly of life, or rather death, in the trenches.

I myself also appeared once more in a minor role as the ghost of Oliver Cromwell, and I still remember my indignation at a brief rebuke in the *The Stage* as having made far too much noise. It was an unfair rebuke – the noise was caused by someone ordering me the wrong size bootees.

However, the national press took us up with a vengeance. Controversy raged on page one. Illustrious ex-warriors and leading bishops were canvassed for their opinions on the propriety of the forthcoming arrangements. Here was unexpected fame for all of us, we decided. The production was scheduled to move directly from Leamington Spa to the West End. The company had thrown a double six and then another. We were euphoric – up the ladders and ignore the snakes. We were to win the game long before most of us had hoped or even dreamed of recognition or fame.

Even an unfortunate gaffe of my own was forgiven. I was dispatched post haste to the local gramophone shop to secure a record of the "Hallelujah Chorus", to be played while the cathedral pillars were being sited behind the safety curtain. But I returned with Ethel Merman belting out "Hallelujah, I'm a Bum" from the popular musical *Hit The Deck*.

Such was our notoriety that the London critics, never very keen to leave the environs of the West End, journeyed to Leamington Spa. On the first night of *The Eternal Flame* they strained first their ears and then their imaginations, waiting rather impatiently for the sensation of the evening. Finally the Unknown Soldier was disclosed, stepping, on this occasion, not through the mud but through a gigantic wreath of poppies. He did not fulfil everyone's expectation of the masculine virility required for the role. The critics went to town, or at least made their way to the nearest telephone box, and any hope we had held of an immediate move to Drury Lane vanished when we read the notices. Mercifully I remember only one. The headlines read: "ETERNAL TALK IN THE ETERNAL FLAME".

We completed an inglorious week and never saw the author again. Years later he died in a tube train.

Russell resumed the tour of *Doctor Syn*. I asked him months later why he had cast the beautiful but silent young lady as the ingénue.

"Not a strong voice," he replied, "but did you ever see

such a beautiful head of hair?"

He was right, mind you, but unfortunately we weren't playing a mime version of Goldilocks and the Three Bears.

"Famous for Fresh Air and Fun"
BLACKPOOL TOURIST BOARD

Blackpool was indeed my idea of the ideal fun town years before I discovered Las Vegas. It was the most pleasurable date in Britain and pleasure was what it catered for. On the Monday, when we arrived in town with a tour, we applied for free tickets to the circus, the Tower Ballroom and complimentary admittance to any other attraction playing there. Entertainments were administered by the Council, along with the three nineteenth-century piers, the sands which formed the forty-acre pleasure beach and the deck-chairs. In autumn the trams were disguised as floating swans and we rode them to admire the illuminations. Professionals arrived from all over Europe to carry off a never-ending series of trophies awarded for ballroom dancing. Not that I ever entered, but I was once tapped on the shoulder by a dance marshal who breathed the word, "Nicer," into my ear. If I hugged my partner a shade too closely it was, I am sure, only an effort to keep my balance. But the shame persisted.

In later years I moved up market to Blackpool's more refined neighbour, noted mainly for golf courses, and stayed at Lytham St Annes with the great Marie Tempest, who was performing in one of my plays. In the mornings she took a drive and, returning from it for lunch one day, she expressed her horror at the plight of the Rector of Stiffkey, who had rented a booth among the side-shows of Blackpool and advertised himself as "Roasting in Hell". He wasn't actually a rector any more, as he had been unfrocked after an ecclesiastical court had enquired into his abiding interest in Soho's prostitution circles and the consequent neglect of his own pastoral duties.

"You met him once, Willie," Marie informed her husband. "He was a theatrical chaplain."

"Did you have a peep at his act?" we asked.

"I never touch pitch," was her haughty admonition, "and I trust you never will."

But naturally we did. There he was, smoking a cigar and lying on a bed of flashing red bulbs. He greeted us warmly though he was not, of course, suffering from the heat.

"Your missus was in this morning," he told Willie. "We had ever such a jolly chat."

Later, proving more ambitious, the Rector of Stiffkey played Daniel in the Lion's Den and one afternoon was fatally mauled. He died as he would have liked – making headlines.

"A little work, a little play
To keep us going – and so, good-day!
A little warmth, a little light
Of love's bestowing – and so, good-night!
A little fun, to match the sorrow
Of each day's growing – and so, good-morrow!
A little trust that when we die
We reap our sowing! and so – good-bye!

GEORGE DU MAURIER

The first time I saw Perranporth, where I subsequently spent four hilarious seasons in Peter Bull's Summer Theatre, it was a severe disappointment. The idea was that we should all share premises secured by our impresario. I had imagined a gracious villa overlooking a creek with cedar trees in the garden and green lawns lapped by the gentle waves of traditional Cornwall. The reality turned out to be a flat above a boot shop in the featureless and hideous main street. Whatever made the monk Piran found his monastery here in the first century, giving the town its name, I could not begin to imagine. But then that was before the sands shifted and the boot shop was built.

Peter was my second best friend. I am not sure where I figured on his list, as he had hundreds, possibly thousands whom he kept severely compartmentalized. All his life he was in love, though of course never married as they say in *The Times* obituaries.

We had been rehearsing for some weeks in his mother's enormous house in Cadogan Gardens. Lady Bull was the widow of an eminent Member of Parliament and their three sons shared the premises. Peter's elder brother, Stephen, had inherited the title. Of him great things were expected. He was already, at the time of our rehearsals, walking out, if that is what royalty do, with the daughter of the King of Spain. Whenever I saw him he was dressed in white tie and tails and setting out for a night of revelry which we all assumed was at least a debutante's ball at the Palace. Stephen, however, had a low threshold of boredom. As a prisoner of the Japanese during the war he tired of a forced march and sat under a sheltering tree, where he quietly died.

Peter's second brother, Anthony, was already working his way up the Underground, which he was later to control. In those days the Underground meant simply the Tube and the District Line. He was in the inner circle of London Transport. He was not yet the proud husband of a young bride or the father of a beautiful daughter, who was only a week old when her mother, sitting up in bed and apparently recovering from childbirth, died. Anthony went on running the trains, but his own life was forever derailed.

But all this was in the future and the present was Peter Bull and his summer company rehearsing in Chelsea and staying on for supper.

"I'm afraid there isn't a pudding," Lady Bull confided, "my boys are savoury boys."

Peter inherited not the title but his father's stature. He closely resembled Cyril Connolly and was, like him, a patron of the Fringe. He could indeed claim to have invented fringe theatre at Perranporth. Most of us were destined to do quite well when we reached the centre. It was a fairly self-satisfied company – Pamela Brown, Judith Furse, Roger Furse, Jill Furse, Pauline Letts, Frith Banbury, Richard Ainley – we all thought a lot of ourselves and a good deal of each other.

The inhabitants of the town and the summer visitors were initially surprised when we arrived, but came round to us. They lent us their furniture and then came to admire it on the small stage, until one morning when Richard Ainley, tired of my direction and general bossiness, smashed everything in sight with a cricket stump. After that the locals were loath to part with their Welsh dressers and wheelback chairs.

Peter always maintained that we were eating him out of house and home. He paid for the food and everything else. The profits, which were never very large, were to be distributed when he decided the time had come to pack up. In Perranporth we seemed to exist on boiled eggs, cornish pasties, jellies and tapioca pudding.

The actor Hugh Sinclair and his wife had a house nearby and came dutifully to first nights. Peter could never persuade either of them into making a guest appearance and never quite forgave Hugh's extolling one of his productions as "a really brave effort".

Our first task on the morning after our arrival was to stack the china belonging, as did the hall itself, to the Women's Institute. Then we set up the chairs and opened the box-office. As we became more successful, double bookings became the norm. We were perpetually overbooked and had to refund our audience or try to persuade them to come to a later performance. The reason for this was that we all loved sitting in the sun and accepting compliments from passersby who had enjoyed our previous performances. We dished out the tickets and forgot to mark off the seating plan. Haphazard we may have been, but I have never enjoyed the theatre so much either before or since. It gave us all the chance to star in our turn. Occasionally we did new plays. My own, *Goodness How Sad*, was born there and had a small triumph which was, alas, not to be repeated at the Vaudeville Theatre, when it was directed by Tyrone Guthrie and cost Peter, as the producer, a small fortune. At Perranporth, if we were a little too big for our boots, we could always discard them on the sands and take to the surfboards.

I tried surfing years later one morning in Hawaii. I couldn't even mount the board and returned to find my young daughter in tears.

"People were laughing at you," she sobbed.

"Usually they have to pay to laugh at me," I told her. "Anyway it is a different sort of surf. I managed very well in Perranporth." And I had.

There were four lovely Cornish summers and then the war. Our friendship, Peter's and mine, continued over the years until he died quite young and very suddenly. His health collapsing, he decided it was time to go.

His enthusiasm for life was infectious, though not (as far as I was concerned) his enthusiasm for teddy bears, on which he was recognized as a world authority. His books about them still sell. Aloysius, his favourite, became the star of the televised *Brideshead Revisited*. He always carried miniature bears in his pockets and organized rallies in the Albert Hall.

Once Peter opened a shop, not to sell bears, but astrological books and paraphernalia. The Sultan of Oman became one of his best customers and even consulted the resident soothsayer. Peter's faith in her predictions was sorely tried when she failed to apprise him that his own premises were about to be incinerated, but he never lost faith in the stars.

I shared his love of fishcakes, which he cooked extravagantly, and I was proud that my name was engraved among the countless mugs which adorned his kitchen dresser. No one has ever forgotten Peter or the friendship he afforded to so many. He died of cardiac arrest – the staunchest heart I ever encountered.

"The movies are the only business where you can go out front and applaud yourself."

WILL ROGERS

Today Denham is noted mainly for the roundabout marking the beginning of the M40 motorway. Once it was studio city. In 1935 Alexander Korda had found 165 acres of meadows, forests and lakes; there was even a river on the premises, the Colne, winding through the flora. The property was called The Fishery and Korda turned the old house into the studio headquarters, the stables became editing-rooms and the gardener's cottage was the music department. Altogether there were seven sound stages, fifteen 'star' dressing-rooms and a studio restaurant complete with Korda's own French chef. The studio, along with the necessary workshops also boasted its own water supply, electric power plant and a zoo.

For me, this story starts not in Buckinghamshire but in Devonshire just two miles north of one of the oldest and indeed most beautiful of English towns, Totnes. The place was Dartington, noted mostly for its educational establishments and it was in the grounds of one of these that we gathered. The director, Gabriel Pascal, had taken us all down to film the exteriors of the last act of *Major Barbara*.

He had cast something of an unknown to play the part of Cusins. Pascal believed in backing outsiders, himself included. I suppose Bernard Shaw thought of him as what Bluntchli might have grown up to become. Gabriel, however, never grew up. He remained a child at play, an *enfant terrible* in the movie world who enjoyed tantrums. He was always the first on the set, shouting at whoever was nearest. "You are crucifying me," was his constant plaint. He had, as producer and director, charge of the nursery in which no one was allowed to put the toys away. He would shoot a scene forty times, complaining, "The last was not good for me." Something always offended. Often a harmless spectator behind the camera had distracted his attention at a critical point in the action. His aides, a formidable combination of Neame and Lean, would assure him that an extra blowing his nose was not actually on camera.

"No good for me," he would reiterate and take forty-five would commence.

Not surprisingly, he took nine months to shoot a picture. It was long enough for me to buy a house and my wife to have our first child. He was often on the telephone to my agent complaining of my performance and urging that his client should take a cut.

"If Morley is as bad as you say," my agent replied, "he would be very unwise to take a cut in salary as obviously he will never work again. I must advise him to make hay while the sun shines."

The sun seldom shone that summer in Devonshire. It rained incessantly and Pascal had us all in the school library reading the play over and over again. He taught me how to light a cigar, but took a whole day doing so and finally I could only complete the process when he removed himself from the set and my hand stopped shaking. His scapegoat, however, was not me but the actor he had cast as Cusins, who was bullied unmercifully. Once I advised him to strike

TAKE 39 and still serene

back.

"You are the star," I urged him, "behave like one."

Not for the first time my advice proved fatal.

"When you read like that," Pascal told him, "it is all grey, like the clouds outside."

"A very pretty colour," he retorted.

"Not good for me," was the inevitable comment.

Pascal sacked him, abandoned the shoot, returned to Denham and cast Rex Harrison to play Cusins.

"He is exactly right for the part," he explained for my benefit. "Rex has the face of a tortured Christ."

But David Lean, who knew *he* couldn't be replaced because Pascal never knew exactly how to position his camera or shoot a scene, agreed on this occasion, but added cynically, "Tortured of course by too tight shoes."

Rex was, however, uncannily good in the part. The other actor never reproached me and went on to have a very successful life as a BBC producer. The picture turned out quite well too, although a good deal of the drama took place behind the camera. One day Pascal's principal backer, Oscar Deutsch paid us a visit presumably to ascertain for himself what was holding up the proceedings. The set was the Salvation Army shelter, dominated by an enormous steel pipe. Deutsch, sitting in the customary canvas seat on which his name had been hastily stencilled, watched while it was dismembered to facilitate the entrance of a crane. Pascal was in a strange mood.

"Cut and print," he ordered to our amazement on the first take.

The next task was to replace the pipe and it was a task which proved insuperable. There were no more scenes completed that day. On that day too, I think, Deutsch discovered where his money had gone. Nevertheless the guarantee for the "end money" was forthcoming, though it proved inadequate to complete the production. We finished the picture in the humbler surroundings of the studios' own boiler-room.

It wasn't, of course, all Pascal's fault. The authorities had decided to commandeer some of the Denham facilities to establish a small explosives factory for the war effort. As a consequence, whenever a solitary aeroplane crossed over the White Cliffs of Dover and even before it could be identified as belonging to the enemy, the alarm sounded and the cast and film crew took to the shelters. Tired of sitting around on benches, I suggested to Wendy Hiller, who was playing the title role, that she should tackle Gabriel for permission to share his own shelter.

"It's under the lake," I told her, "and exquisitely furnished with deep leather armchairs."

When the all clear sounded, she pleaded with him for cast equality. Pascal thought she had gone mad. There was a lake, in point of fact, but no shelter under it and certainly no leather armchairs. Wendy was not pleased at being duped, but it was one of my happiest days.

"The true artist will let his wife starve, his children go barefoot, his mother drudge for her living at seventy, sooner than work at anything but his art."

G. B. SHAW

Gabriel Pascal's life sounded like a fantasy worthy of Baron Munchausen himself. His early days, he told us, were spent as a carpet seller in reduced circumstances in Zanzibar. Then he commanded a crack Hungarian regiment. On his arrival in England, the myth had it that he arrived on Bernard Shaw's doorstep with only a half-crown in his pocket and managed to secure the film rights to all of Shaw's plays. There must have been some truth in the last claim: Shaw visited us often on the set. Once, watching a scene from his masterpiece, he commiserated with the players.

"Nothing much you can do with that one," he told us. "It has always been a terrible last act."

Korda, another Hungarian émigré, was reported to have once admonished a member of his family. "It is not enough just to be a Hungarian in Britain these days. You have to be clever too."

Gabriel Pascal, however, relied on his own performance as the British conception of the archetypal central European. What you had to be was outrageous. His performance at Denham that year was one of the best I have ever seen – on screen or off.

"I loathe abroad, nothing would induce me to live there . . . and, as for foreigners, they are all the same, and they all make me sick."

NANCY MITFORD, *The Pursuit of Love*

It was a mistake to try and persuade Nancy Mitford that she was enjoying her stay on tour with *The Little Hut*. She had translated it and adapted it from the French by André Roussin. It was her first foray into the theatrical world – a world she soon discovered she didn't like. Besides that, she was missing her beloved Paris. She hated Britain and didn't like touring her own play.

Driving from Blackpool (where I tried to teach her to roller skate) to Harrogate, we paused at Castle Howard, the vast baroque mansion built by Sir John Vanbrugh. He drew up the first plans for it in 1699 and, when he died in 1726, he was still working on the building. Nancy was not impressed. She virtually ignored the Rubens in the Orleans room, the Holbeins and Van Dykes in the Long Gallery and the Burne-Jones stained glass in the chapel.

"I would like to speak to the curator," she informed the

attendant and, when he arrived, she chided him on the inclusion of a china plate.

"Not Sèvres," she informed him. "It is an obvious fake."

We left the discomfited curator and resumed our journey.

"I do happen to know about china," she told me. "The countess with whom I stay in the summer to write my books has the finest collection of Sèvres in France – possibly the world. It was inherited from her dead son, of course. They shot him in the war."

"The Germans?" I enquired.

"I don't suppose so," she said matter-of-factly, "most likely a fellow officer. He was discovered to be homosexual, but was allowed to return home to procreate. As soon as his wife conceived they posted him to the front line and advised him to get himself shot at his earliest convenience. When the child was born, of course, it was a girl. Even the French can't manage everything. The title lapsed and his mother turned to religion. She prays incessantly and there is always a priest for the masses and cardinals for dinner. Well, at least bishops."

"I think that is a terrible story," I told her.

"Why terrible?" she wondered. "Disappointing perhaps."

Nothing shocked Nancy, I thought then – but Mr Cornelius was to prove the exception. By this time we had reached Harrogate and I was cruising the 200-acre common known as the Strays, wondering where we should lodge. I stopped the car beside a seat on which I spied a gentleman with boned shoes – surely a reliable informant. He turned out to be Mr Cornelius, who was not only respectable it seemed but was even a member of my father-in-law's club, Bucks.

"Try the Grand," he told us, "and while you are about it you might care to dine with me there."

It was a spectacular meal. Grouse, naturally, this being moors country, and extravagant wines. Our host abstained from the wines. He was after all drawn to Harrogate, the north's most popular spa town with its ninety sulphur and iron springs, to take the cure. So he drank only whiskey and rationed himself to a bottle a day.

Hospitality I decided had to be returned. The least we could do, I urged Nancy, was to offer him a box at the Grand Theatre in Leeds, where we were playing, and of course supper afterwards.

"I shall leave the arrangements to you," I told her. "After all, in your case grouse is no problem. We are practically neighbours of your brother-in-law, Devonshire."

"Andrew's birds are born with a Sainsbury label round their necks," she said, "but I'll do my best."

Nancy proceeded in her aristocratic style to arrange the dinner. That was when Mr Cornelius shocked her to the quick.

"Can you imagine," the inventor of U and non-U told me, "the brute has just rung up and asked to bring the hotel manicurist? He must think he is moving in theatrical circles."

"He is," I reminded her. "I don't understand the problem. His Grace told you he was sending a couple of brace. There'll be plenty of grouse for all."

Nancy remained outraged. In the end the old gentleman's companion stood him up, but the party remained subdued. Just the idea of such a social *faux pas* ruined the evening for Nancy. The man was obviously not what he seemed.

The play moved on to Newcastle and a week later, at the Railway Hotel there, Nancy was equally reticent when her father invited us to dine after the performance.

"I don't know what we'll get to eat," the noted eccentric remarked as we took our seats. "These sons of monkeys," here he courteously indicated the head waiter who hovered, "go to bed at midnight. Have you read her books?" he demanded of me in the same breath. "Of course my daughter doesn't know the difference between a hunting crop and a riding whip."

Nancy remained silent throughout.

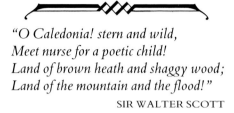

In Tobermory they induced Nathalie Delon to dive into the waves. Too late they discovered a plastic cup floating nearby. "Just once more," they begged her, but they had to wait. We were shooting the film in colour and she had turned bright blue.

When not filming, we lived in holiday villas among the gorse and were eaten alive by midges. The director was French and cooked for his loyal crew and not quite so loyal cast when night fell. We were entertained at the local castle by Her Majesty's Court Chamberlain, who was most proud of an eventful career in which he had succeeded in dressing boy scouts in long trousers.

"Saved a good deal of trouble," he opined.

Chapped knees, I imagined.

In one scene I was supposed to fire a revolver at Jack Hawkins, who played a villainous sea captain bent on ramming my cockleshell.

"How do you fire this thing?" I enquired of Miss Delon.

If there was one thing we were supposed never to mention to her it was guns, owing to a recent fatal shooting vaguely connected with her bodyguard. I was still blushing when the camera hove to and focused. You can't win them all, but I much preferred the mainland and a sumptuous hotel at the Kyle of Lochalsh.

I was no stranger to embarrassment in Scotland. One very early morning in my youthful touring days I was returning to my digs having had a triumphant night cuckolding the leading man and the proprietor of the production, who was admittedly away raising money for the disastrous enterprise. Taking unfair advantage, I had come and seen and conquered – even my own tendency for premature ejaculation. Edinburgh in the moonlight had never seemed more beautiful, the old part of the city never more deserted. I was suddenly aware of danger. Behind me shuffling footsteps were gaining. Was it the husband? I looked over my shoulder. A figure in rags pursued. His feet were turned outwards, cloth where there should have been boots. Man or ghost? I have never been able to decide. All I did decide was to run faster than I had ever run before or since. Somehow I managed to outspeed my spectral mugger.

Edinburgh in those days supported an exciting night life and two dance clubs with professional hostesses. For a fee you could book them out for the evening. I considered myself to be in love with a girl called Dolly, but found booking her out didn't include booking her into bed. I wrote to her after the tour moved on and only ceased correspondence when a lurid account in the *News of the World* announced that the club proprietors were charged with operating a vice ring.

Years afterwards, on the eve of a pre-West End try-out of my first play, to which I had invited my mother and a couple of aunts, the phone in my bedroom rang and Dolly congratulated me. Had she kept my letters, I wondered, and panicked.

"I'm not that Robert Morley," I told her. "I believe there is an actor with a similar name."

"How strange," she told me. "In the photograph in the *Scotsman* you look amazingly like the Robert Morley I knew."

Storm tossed trio (with Nathalie Delon and Anthony Hopkins)

I hung up agreeing it was something of a coincidence.

On the first night Dolly appeared and introduced her husband, an eminent surgeon: "But of course you are not the Robert Morley I used to know."

I floundered and quickly agreed.

"If you should ever meet him," she went on, "just give him my regards and tell him never to forget old friends."

Mother joined me on the staircase. "Who were they?" she asked. "Such an elegant couple!"

"Just fans," I replied. The danger had passed but the memory lingers. Perhaps it doesn't pay to be over-cautious.

Glasgow is now the showpiece of Scotland. I remember the old days and Sauchiehall Street, The Gorbals and the hospital. Shown round the latter, I asked a doctor about his strangest patient.

"We had a fellow once we treated for a poisoned hand," he told me. "None of us understood his complaint, but an old porter, who had been here for years, enlightened us a bit too late. 'How's your leprosy case coming along?' he enquired. 'You managed to cure him I hope.' We had, I'm afraid, sent him back to India no better. Leprosy was fairly common among seamen who turned up here years ago, but none of us youngsters had ever seen a case."

In those days we played Aberdeen and Dundee. The Scots had discovered marmalade then, but not yet oil, which is why I imagine we didn't ever manage to fill the houses. Harry Lauder never had that problem. When you heard him singing, "Keep right on to the end of the road", you sensed what Scotland was all about.

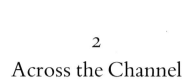

2
Across the Channel

*Europe is full of temptations (with George Segal and
Jacqueline Bisset)*

2
ACROSS THE
CHANNEL

"Life is too short to learn German."
RICHARD PORSON

I WAS DISAPPOINTED in luncheon: whipped cream with a cherry on top is not suitable nourishment for a growing man and I supposed I was still growing. At sixteen I had come to Hanover to learn the language and learned not to order *shlag zahne* simply because it was the cheapest item on the menu. Even the waiter seemed mildly surprised.

He'll just have to imagine I'm on some sort of diet, I told myself and saved the cherry till last. I don't imagine cream had been on the menu for long. There had been famine abroad and even bandits.

"One of us sat up at night," my host assured me.

Things were better now. The mark was devalued and stabilized. My host was a bank manager and, unlike the ones at home, he worked right through the weekend. He was never too tired in the evenings to correct my grammar.

"*Das geht nicht,*" he would interpolate whenever I tried to complete a sentence.

There was a son of the house who was always trying to get his face slashed in a duel. It was a status symbol for students.

"You should try it," he urged.

I am a natural coward who always used to jump if I saw a hockey ball coming towards the goalpost I was supposed to defend. Here they rubbed salt or something into the wounds to perpetuate the scars. It was not for me.

Field Marshal von Hindenburg lived up the road. Daily and punctually he paraded in the park, and there was always a small group of spectators lined up as if to glimpse the Queen in the Royal Enclosure; the numbers were fewer, however.

Herr Prasuhn, my host, was keen on mystery tours. At least they were a mystery to me as I never grasped whither we were bound. One day it turned out to be a riding display at the military barracks, where I had the pleasure of my first erotic experience, appreciating a schoolgirl in a short navy blue pleated skirt behaving like a cossack. I was, it is true, a late developer, but in Hanover there was an adolescent Brünhilde who courted me. I used to have to take her dancing and she always ordered the most expensive ice-creams, which she never ate.

"I am much too much in love with you, Herr Robert," she would remark.

"In that case give it to me," I told her and gobbled up the knickerbocker glory.

One day her brother called and challenged me. It was a question of sabres or marriage. Steeled by the thought of what mother would have said if I had returned with a genuine Rhine maiden, I called his bluff.

"*War is the national industry of Prussia.*"

COMTE DE MIRABEAU

It was not only the students who were thirsty for blood in Hanover in those days. Herr Prasuhn and I spent a long evening peering through the shutters of an abandoned butcher's shop. Here had operated the first recorded serial killer. Later the tree trunks were decorated with a photograph and a statement of execution. My host, who seemed to be the kindest of men, also took me motor racing and was seriously disappointed by the lack of a fatality.

"Last week, when you didn't come, there were *drei tods,*" he told me.

I had to ask for food in the native tongue during my sojourn. *"Bitte,* a slice of ham," I would demand.

"Das geht nicht," was the inevitable reply and the platter never came my way. There was also a good deal of forced geniality. Good appetite had to be wished before starting to eat. If I forgot – no food. I used to be quite hungry at times. I was also, of course, extremely lonely. There wasn't another Englishman abroad, at least not in Hanover.

On the day Hindenburg was elected president we saw him off at the railway station.

"Das geht nicht," remarked Herr Prasuhn. *"Er ist schrechlich alt."* Or words to that effect.

"So," I replied boldly adding a new word to my vocabulary, *"naturlich."*

I never did learn German.

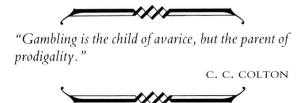

"Gambling is the child of avarice, but the parent of prodigality."

C. C. COLTON

At sixteen I knew very little about myself. I didn't even know for sure that I was part of my father's plot to rob the bank and escape to Monte Carlo. He had persuaded the family he needed capital to take me to Tours and settle me down to learn French. Arriving rather late in the day, we gave the place a cursory inspection. All seemed quiet at the railway station. Father ordered me a hock and seltzer at the

buffet, and went off to make enquiries. He came back with
the address of a small hotel nearby and a list of the train times
to Monte. Next morning we strolled to a local bridge and
Father sniffed the water.

"I don't think you would be happy here, Bobby," he said.
"In France one is safer by the sea."

We lunched on *bouillabaisse*. Eating up the scraps, Father
observed then that we were off to "Monsieur le professeur".
He lived in a rather neat villa outside town. The road was
signposted *"Vers l'abatoir"*.

"I don't like the look of this," remarked my father. "It
could be dangerous. He never told me he was near the
slaughterhouse." He looked round cautiously. "You don't
like horses."

As if on cue a solitary rider appeared. He seemed well
turned out and was wearing a top hat. We watched him pass
at a sedate trot.

"Poor brute," exclaimed Papa.

"Why do you suppose he's wearing a top hat?" I enquired.

"Dressed for the horse's funeral," he explained.

We had yet to approach the professor's house. "Are we
going in?" I asked.

"I don't think so. I think we have seen enough," Father
said. "Besides, we don't want to miss the train."

It would be easy to dismiss Father as being only really at
peace while the ball was spinning around the wheel on the
roulette table, although in all occupations he was disaster
prone. Shortly before the Boer War broke out he had
resigned his commission, but retained his ceremonial helmet,
which graced the dining-room table: it was used as a biscuit
tin, but was not, alas, airtight enough to preserve the
contents. He had also published at his own expense a poem
which he advertised in *The Times* as obtained by sending a
pound to the poet. The blurb stated that he had discovered

the certainty of an after life.

"It's extraordinary," he told me, "how few seem really interested in what, after all, must provide an answer to the world's greatest conundrum."

The poem itself did little to solve the riddle. It was a sentimental account of an Edwardian wedding at which the bride held a bouquet of violets which miraculously lasted when the marriage packed up.

Lest it be thought that Father spent his whole life gambling (which he did), there were times when he tried hard to accumulate the cash to finance his external journeys from casinos to race meetings to dog tracks to poker clubs. In the First World War he returned to the colours. Not to those of the Dragoons, but taking on a less dashing role as guardian of a railway tunnel outside Three Bridges, Kent. No serious attempt having been made to blow up the structure, he quitted his post and with the help of Lord Cowdray, opened a club for Air Force officers next to the Cavalry in Piccadilly. He became secretary and then took on a similar post at Boodles. His patience was sorely tried, however, by the insistence of members in dating his waitresses. This led to continual depletion of the staff. Each year, when the premises shut for the summer vacation, he appropriated the money left in the safe, judging it safer in his own pocket. It never was, of course, so towards the end of August he would take to his bed with a revolver under the pillows. He would disclose the weapon to his visiting relatives and, long before Hitler coined the phrase, indicate that the gun was the final solution . . . unless of course someone could be persuaded to come up with the money he owed – preferably in fivers.

The relatives, suitably convinced that he really would kill himself this time, invariably came up with the cash. Mission accomplished he would rise from his bed, lock away the gun (until the next time) and repair to the club to welcome members to the bridge table.

But, to return to my first visit to Monte Carlo, though not of course my parent's: he had, indeed, succeeded in spending his honeymoon there, although he had faithfully promised his father-in-law, who had been persuaded to settle his liabilities, never to gamble again.

I found the principality a great deal sunnier and more comfortable than Tours. In the immediate proximity of a casino Father became a first-class citizen. There was to be no more *bouillabaisse*. I supposed, though, that as a student I would not continue to board at the Hôtel de Paris and feast on champagne and caviar. But Father, having robbed the family of one bank, was intent on robbing another. Nothing worried him – not even his piles. In the daytime he sported spotless white trousers reminding me only occasionally of the greatest trauma of my school days. There had been a parents' shooting match with the senior boys. Father had lain on his stomach and a small spot of blood was revealed on his buttocks. I have never forgotten the awfulness of that afternoon, but yet I cannot exactly remember what Monte Carlo was like on my first visit. There were still grand dukes roaming the Casino Gardens and Father was never tired of praising the flower beds. In those days there was an atmosphere of cloistered happiness.

At breakfast Father read *Sporting Life,* three days out of date. He read it without turning the pages upside down as was his custom at home. He had been quite badly wounded in South Africa, where the surgeons had shrunk from extracting a bullet which was judged to be close to his heart. They adjured him to avoid excitement in the future. Consequently he always closed his eyes as the horse approached the winning post and when he was not present at the track, reversed the stop press column in the evening newspaper to avoid excessive stimulation out of a fear that the missile might suddenly shift.

In the daytime, before the casino opened its doors, Father

immersed himself in the legends and poetry of the little town and, when he was not inspecting deserted villas, he was an indefatigable guide. We viewed the small terrace where an earlier player had coated himself with blood, or possibly some other red substance, turned his pockets inside out and discharged a revolver loaded with blanks. The casino authorities, fearing bad publicity, supplied a substantial wad of bank notes, which they placed in his pockets before alerting the police. The solitary casino employee left guarding the corpse while the gendarmerie were fetched fainted (or more probably was bribed so to do) and the corpse, making a miraculous recovery, disappeared.

On another morning we found ourselves at the bar of the golf club awaiting the arrival of the secretary. He, alas, had other business to attend to and never appeared.

"Were you thinking of joining?" I asked my father. It would have been a surprising move since, as far as I knew, my father had never swung a club.

"No, I just thought you would like to meet him," he explained on the way back to the hotel. "You see, Bobby, he was the man who broke the bank."

His story inspired my father. It seems that one morning at the roulette table only the first dozen numbers had turned up consecutively for half an hour. He had made a fortune and left vowing never to return. Of course, the same evening he was back instructing the croupier to stake the maximum on number eight. The over-zealous croupier interpreted his wishes as including not only that number itself but also every other combination on the wheel which included eight. Obligingly the ball settled on eight. Play was suspended temporarily while fresh counters were obtained. This time my father's hero took off on a voyage around the world. Some five years later he returned and having spent his fortune, happily accepted the offer of the authorities to manage the golf course.

"If yet thou love game at so dear a rate,
Learn this, that hath old gamesters dearly cost:
Dost lose? rise up; dost win? rise in that state.
Who strive to sit out losing hands are lost."

GEORGE HERBERT

Three days into our visit it was decided that the simplest way for me to acquire the French tongue would be for Father to buy a villa somewhere along the coast, where he would would install a professor to keep me company. He planned on installing also a number of other students, who, unlike me, would be fee paying. There would, of course, also be certain advantages to himself in acquiring a *pied à terre* in the district.

"You understand that phrase?" he enquired fondly. "Good. Well then, we had better start house hunting."

He found one he thought would be suitable. "This would be your bedroom," he explained as we inspected the property. "But, of course, you might have to share. I think we could do with ten students, at least to start with. There are only four bedrooms, it is true, but the professor would sleep out. Would you mind that?"

"I don't know," I told Father, "I haven't met him."

Nor, of course, had Father. "No, no," he explained, "I meant would you mind sharing a bedroom? It is a nice house, quite. The only trouble is the French will insist on building next to the railway line, but I don't think there are all that many trains and they do say that after a time you don't notice them at all."

Fortunately we were able to notice the one which bore us home the very next morning. We travelled back third class. Dreams of language schools had been abandoned or at least temporarily shelved. Father's disastrous night at the casino had exhausted all available cash and far worse; he had drawn a cheque on his English bank, in which he very well knew there was no money. In France it is a criminal offence to write cheques when no funds are available. Father faced the awful threat of being excluded forever from French casinos. We were speeding homewards somehow to repair the breach. In the meanwhile Father was in black despair.

"Thank God you were with me, old man," Father said. "I might otherwise have gone for an early morning swim."

His tone was ominous but this mood improved noticeably at Folkestone, where the races had already started and we found we were in time for the last four. We then went on to the dog track at White City and Father's luck took a turn for the better.

"There you are. You see," Father told me, "to accumulate you must speculate."

I'm not sure if Father ever returned to Monte Carlo, but I have been fortunate enough to do so often. There is always the chance that the bank will once again be broken – and it could be my turn to learn golf.

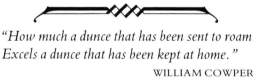

*"How much a dunce that has been sent to roam
Excels a dunce that has been kept at home."*
WILLIAM COWPER

I spent a few happy weeks in the charming Italian coastal resort of Alassio, in the province of Savona. Father was still keen on my learning a foreign language, still planning to send me *en route* to the diplomatic service. I found Alassio had a slightly more attractive ambience than Tours. I can't pretend to have learned much Italian – I can't pretend to have learned any, in point of fact. I was the sole pupil of an English colonel who had recently opened a sort of crammers and spoke not a word of the language himself. We were attended at times by one of the natives, who attempted to instruct us in the lingo. The Colonel's attitude, like mine, was that, if people couldn't speak English, that was too bad – for them, of course. Fortunately there were quite a lot of our fellow countrymen in Alassio then, behaving as I imagine an earlier generation had comported themselves in Poona. The high street was always referred to by us as the "Main Drain". Going native was frowned upon. We were not encouraged to dance with Italian girls or even escort them to the tennis club, where weekly hops took place on Saturday evenings. Segregation was the rule on the courts, too, where Italians were not only notoriously unsporting but also played better tennis.

I was under the impression that the British were only happy abroad when the natives were waiters. (I later found this observation of mine quoted in a collection of aphorisms to my undying pride.)

It was there I first met Leslie Clark, a high official in the Harmsworth Press, whom I greatly admired and who encouraged me to become a journalist. There I fell in love with a girl who lived with a rather bohemian family. Her father was an earlier version of Lawrence Durrell. On one occasion the Colonel interrupted us playing tennis and complained that I had used his lavatory and forgotten to pull the chain. He dispatched me forthwith to do just that. I have had a phobia ever since, often returning unnecessarily to the bathroom to ensure that I have flushed. So I suppose my time in Italy was not entirely wasted.

After this occasion my resentment smouldered. I quarrelled increasingly with my tutor until one day, losing patience, he told me that I was such an idiot that any further attempt to tutor me was a waste of his time and my parents' money. I was not slow in communicating his verdict. Father instantly stopped paying and I left for home. As there were no longer likely pupils in sight, the Colonel for his part stopped paying the rent and closed down the villa. So, in a way, I had the last word, but alas not in Italian.

When I told Father about the meeting with Leslie Clark and his judgement that I should be a journalist, he got me an interview with Lord Astor, who owned *The Times.* I never met anyone with more charm and such a total appreciation of my needs. After a short time he rang the bell for the managing editor and instructed him to engage me on the spot. How right, I thought, was Papa's belief that it was always better to start at the top. A few days later I received a sympathetic letter from one of his staff explaining that it was not the usual practice for *The Times* to take on beginners and offering me an introduction to the *Enfield Courier*, where there might be an early vacancy to report on local events. I never availed myself of the opening and reverted to my earlier ambition to try the theatre.

When I went back to Alassio many years later, it seemed to have recovered from my sudden departure and become exceedingly prosperous. The locals had taken to entrapping my fellow citizens in high-rise hotels built on the sand and on the fortunes to be made from package holidays. The English Library and the English Church had vanished. Germans sunned themselves on the beach. Only the waiters were still kept busy. I wondered if Poona had followed suit.

"The luxurious capital of the Riviera of Flowers enjoys a delightfully warm temperature and the highest average sunshine in Liguria. These advantages, together with its race course and its gay and brilliant festivals, make it a resort of worldwide repute. Near the Casino is the Corso dell'Imperatrice, famous for its Canary palms."

MICHELIN GUIDE

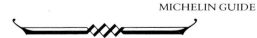

The last time I visited the Italian Riviera it was to stay in its capital, San Remo. It is the largest and oldest winter health resort in Italy, and I was in the company of my father-in-law, Herbert Buckmaster, who wished to consult the greatest authority of the day about his arthritis. The surgeon took one look at the X-rays and then passed them to me with the same verdict as that reached earlier in London by Mr Fox: the case was hopeless and, of course, hip replacement had not yet been thought of – at least by him. His advice was that we return home at once.

Buck gave a farewell dinner party in an effort to use up all the caviar he had had flown in from London. James Stewart (not the actor, but the then chairman of the Conservative Party) was half an hour late. Buck pretended the delicacy had all been consumed and waited his guest's discomfiture. But, when his host produced his portion, James confessed he never touched the stuff and ordered his customary *prosciutto*. He was a delightful character who drank whisky at all hours except at four thirty precisely, when he ordered a cup of tea and tipped what remained of his glass into it. Half an hour later the sun continued to blaze down, but James maintained that it was past the yard arm.

My father-in-law, with increasing pain, grew occasionally choleric. I never heard him so angry as when my friend Sewell Stokes remarked that the then Prime Minister, Harold Macmillan, had been cuckolded over the years by Bob Boothby.

"Not only are they members of my club," Buck rebuked Sewell, "but both are personal friends. I would have been the first to hear. You are committing a grave slander."

A few days later Sewell received a letter of apology offering to make him an honorary member of Buck's Club. "I shall look forward to your acceptance," Buck added. "There is nothing I enjoy these days more than a good gossip."

Buck was a delightful character who ran his club with great regard for his staff, particularly his cook, who specialized in providing the most delicious nursery-type food. It reminded members of their happy formative years. Occasionally the cook threatened to resign.

"That would be," Buck was wont to observe, "the supreme tragedy of my life."

He tolerated the members and there were always a number of people waiting to join. They were a mixed bag of politicos and dukes.

"I shall shoot till Christmas," one of the latter was heard to remark when asked about his future plans once the war had been declared. "Then I shall probably let them give me a job in the War House."

Buck's praise was always reserved for his staff. Only once did I hear him drop a harsh word about them.

"Everything happens to me," he once complained, "now my secretary is going blind."

He conceived the idea of the club while serving in the trenches with fellow officers of the Blues during the First World War.

"I thought it might be nice," he said, "if we could meet later in more congenial circumstances."

His marriage to Gladys Cooper ended and he married another musical-comedy leading lady. When she died, he decided to elope to South Africa with the wife of a leading and somewhat belligerent captain – not of his old regiment, but of industry. Learning in Cape Town that the captain had threatened to shoot him, he finally disembarked at Tilbury with his coat collar turned up and his hat turned down. His face was swathed in a scarf as well, but no bullet awaited. Later, at Ascot with the lady, she was ostentatiously saluted by a stranger who bowed and raised his hat in a manner which Buck considered to be over effusive.

"Who was that cad?" he demanded and was informed it

was the erstwhile marksman.

Many years later, old and increasingly crippled and frail, he was staying with his daughter and myself in the country, and expressed himself puzzled why John, my chauffeur and dresser, wore what seemed to him unsuitable clothing.

"You might at least provide a cap with a cockade," he chided.

One evening he summoned my faithful friend to his bedroom.

"Tomorrow," he told John, "we are going off on a long cruise aboard my boat. When you have dropped Mr Morley at the stage door, make your way to Gieves in Bond Street and get them to kit you out properly. Tell them to send the bill to me."

Luckily I was able to dissuade John from any such foolishness.

"I very much doubt," I told him, "that he still has an account there. Anyway, he lost his boat in enemy action at Frinton."

The next morning Buck slept on. Unable to wake him, we summoned the doctor.

"He will die about four-thirty," the doctor told us.

Buck, punctual as always, did precisely that.

"We are so made that we can derive intense enjoyment from a contrast and very little from a state of things."

SIGMUND FREUD

The only reason I was in Austria was to make a moving picture. Locations are not always bread and honey. The satisfaction of being paid to travel is often eroded by the hours you are expected to perform. It is no good longing for the twilight, as work doesn't necessarily stop even then. The film was called *The Journey*. We seemed, as is so often the case in the industry, to have arrived at the wrong time. Snow was needed to cover the fields as we sped along in the bus. We had to bring it with us, stuck to cardboard, and positioning it took forever. Jason Robards was in a state of continuous celebration, so the local inns were off limits to all but the director. He was not a very endearing character who tended to criticize. Anne Jackson became a lifelong friend of mine; Yul Brynner really did munch wine glasses, and Deborah Kerr, in spite of the script, was destined to fall in love with and eventually marry its author.

The Imperial positively shone and moreover it was constantly being redecorated by my children who bought large quantities of gas-filled balloons from the Prater and let them loose at the very base of the grand staircase to be constantly retrieved by the staff balancing precariously on step-ladders.

There were two small children in the picture. One was a brilliant actor who accepted pubescence when the time came and got a job as an airline steward. The other, Ron Howard, whom no one seemed to notice and who had to be urged on by his parents to perform rather unwillingly, grew up to become a world-famous director and producer. Come to think of it, Jason Robards grew up too.

Fairly late in the shoot I became obsessed with a longing to spot wild turkey. Enlisting the support of David Kossoff, we took off from Vienna for the Hungarian border. I cannot explain my desire to see a wild turkey as I am not at all attracted by flocks of the domestic variety, which seem to me in a state of perpetual panic. On this occasion it was we who panicked, coming unexpectedly as we did on the local killing fields and finding ourselves faced with barbed wire and an observation post from which the guard took a pot shot. We dropped to the ground and then scurried for cover. I suppose it is just possible that the fellow wasn't after us at all. Perhaps he had spotted one of the birds and fancied it for the pot. It didn't seem so at the time.

"I do not want Michael Angelo for breakfast . . . for luncheon – for dinner – for tea – for supper – for between meals . . . Lump the whole thing! Say the Creator made Italy from designs by Michael Angelo."

MARK TWAIN

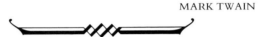

The first time I saw Rome it was too much for me. Am I the only one not to be able to contemplate a Roman bath with pleasure? I dislike all ruins and dread the moment and the spot where the guide reminds me that here oxen once roasted. Who cares? Besides, my life was already fraught by the circumstances in which I was filming *Potiphar's Wife*. In those days Italians were notoriously poor payers. On the strict instructions of my agent, I collected my money nightly in preparation for the next day's shooting. Compatriots were owed thousands of lira. I persuaded them to stop work until they were paid. One of the performers played his last scene with re-inforced calves caused by wadges of money stuffed down his stockings. His elderly parent was thrown down the staircase when he tried the same tactic. You had to choose your moment when demanding money if you wished to avoid becoming suddenly expendable.

The Italians were a ruthless lot, particularly when it came to the gazelle hunt. I was supposed to appear in this scene, but judged it professional suicide in the unlikely event that the league against cruel sports ever saw it.

"Of course, it won't be a live gazelle," the producers assured me. "There are no gazelles in Rome. There is only one stuffed one. We borrow from the museum."

"And the cheetah?" I asked. "That too is stuffed?"

"You ask the impossible," they scorned. "How can you film a stuffed cheetah hunting? You will have it on a leash."

"Oh, no, I won't," I told them.

They excused me from the set and, when I got back, there was a deathly hush. The cheetah, suffering from glaucoma had sprung and somehow swallowed a wire spring. We waited breathlessly for the beast to pass the coiled wire.

Later, they urged me to set alight my own palace. The curtains, made from nylon, turned instantly to sticky candy. Even later they produced sturdier material and buckets of petrol. There was never a more reluctant arsonist than I. Holding the torch at arm's length I tiptoed round to try and set the home fire burning.

Meeting the Pope was more successful. His Holiness received me in private audience – well, semi-private. There was a brief conversation when I tried to persuade him that I was not an Australian. Subsequently I convinced the cast we had discussed Anna Neagle, at least for a time.

"A man who has not been in Italy is always conscious of an inferiority, from his not having seen what is expected a man should see. The grand object of travelling is to see the shores of the Mediterranean."

SAMUEL JOHNSON

I was given the Black Duke's villa in Ravello and told the tale. The Duke had a penchant for boys and engaged a young chauffeur who gradually robbed him of his wealth. The Duke went blind or nearly so and the chauffeur refused him the money for an operation which would have restored his sight. Now, of course, sadly, he had to be led everywhere.

"By the chauffeur?" I asked.

"I'm not certain," was the reply, "but there's no money

left, so he is forced to let the villa."

Actually he had let it to the film company who had reserved it for Humphrey Bogart, but Bogart preferred the hotel, so Prince Tasco (who was John Huston's location manager on *Beat the Devil*) installed me and my family. The Duke had left us his cook, who specialized in spaghetti soufflés. We were in clover.

I was most surprised when, one day, His Grace appeared for luncheon. He seemed to have recovered his sight, though it was true he sported a glass eye. His saturnine companion, much older than I imagined, came too. I tried as best I could to show my dislike for the latter. It was not a happy occasion, but the Black Duke seemed to enjoy himself and even surrendered the keys of the cellar at the end of an afternoon watching Bogart on a donkey.

Of course I had been handed the wrong end of the stick. Far from driving the car, the Duke's companion, for whom I had shown contempt throughout the luncheon, turned out to be an ambassador.

I became very fond of Prince Tasco but I wasn't so keen on his daughter, whose inattention allowed me to back my beautiful new Jaguar into a lorry.

"I asked you to tell me if there was anything coming," I reminded her.

"But that wasn't coming," she told me. "That was there all the time."

The car was a write off and I never drove another.

The road from Amalfi climbs in hairpin bends up the narrow Dragon Valley planted with grape vines to Ravello. With its alleys, stairways and roofed passages, Ravello, clinging to the steep slopes of Dragon Hill is not really suitable for motor vehicles. It wasn't really suitable for a film location either. We spent a great deal of time and energy pushing a Rolls Royce up hills. Once it got away from us and dived over a cliff, laying waste properties on the way down. Quite a large bill for damages was presented to the film company. What worried me far more was that I was supposed to have been in the car along with Bogart, who had jumped in and out with surprising speed when he discovered that there was no one on the floor of the car to apply the brakes, as he had been promised. If I had been as fleet of foot as Bogart, I would have been in the car too instead of being left panting by the roadside.

"You would have been fine, just fine," Huston assured me as usual. Nothing fazed our director.

I was several days late reporting for duty having lingered on the Riviera.

"We are not shooting at present," I was informed when I rather shamefacedly arrived. "Truman Capote, who is writing the script, has had to go back to Rome. His raven has refused to speak to him on the phone and he worried that the bird may be sick or pining for him."

Jennifer Jones developed a mild form of alopecia. David Selznick appeared, it seemed from nowhere, and prescribed the cure; Miss Jones must have an entirely new wardrobe to compete with Gina Lollobrigida. Givenchy arrived from Paris with the *toiles,* fitted them personally and was congratulated by David for imaginatively dressing her entirely in white cotton. Givenchy did not correct him and left her entourage coping for the rest of the shoot with safety-pins.

But it was Truman who captured the imagination. His enlistment as script writer occurred rather late in the proceedings and he was anxious to prolong the engagement. He wrote or re-wrote a couple of pages each evening and read them aloud to the astonished cast just before we were due to shoot a scene. His was the most extraordinary voice I ever heard, high pitched and deeply Southern. He was a muscled fairy. I read with fascination everything he wrote – except of course, the script of *Beat the Devil.*

*"The nether sky opens and Europe is disclosed as a
prone and emaciated figure, the Alps shaping like a
backbone, and the branching mountain chains like ribs,
the peninsular plateau of Spain forming a head."*

THOMAS HARDY

"There must be something for me in *Cromwell,*" I told the
producer of the epic about to roll.

"I don't think so," he replied, "otherwise I would have
noticed. Anyway, come in if you are passing."

I arrived rather too late for a major role, it seemed.

"You can be Manchester," he told me. "He was a duke.
Not a good part, but it goes through. Mostly in Parliament,
but you start in Spain, in Pamplona."

The origins of Pamplona are rooted in Roman times, when
it is said that the city was founded by Pompey. It is the capital
of the ancient Kingdom of Navarre and stands on rising
ground – a broad valley among the Pyrenean foothills.
Luckily, when I arrived, it was not the time of the fiesta of
San Fermin. The side streets were not barricaded nor were
the bulls running. There we were treated to good hotels, but
you had to be ready to move if Richard Harris (who was
Cromwell) showed. In his early days he meant trouble, and
these were his early days. There were rows in the dining-
room and scuffles in the bar.

We spent our time on the plains and in the rain. Mighty
battles were to be enacted. They were performed mostly by
the Spanish cavalry, but some of the British had to be
mounted, myself included. Now, Spanish steeds are trained
to react instantly when the reins are checked. They rear up
and fall over backwards, pretending to be shot.

I kept the reins pretty loose and contented myself with the
instructions, "Whoa there boy. Steady the Buffs." I hoped

they would understand from the tone of my voice.

Arriving after the others in shot, I left a tiresome gap for the cameraman. The others had already practised riding in the Row. Timothy Dalton was particularly vexed. He was always too far ahead with a spaniel balanced on the saddle.

During one wait, while the clouds closed in, the crew covered the camera and withdrew. I sat astride fearing I might not manage to remount. When they returned there were cries of complaint from the operator.

"Who has been messing about?" he demanded. "Morley is now out of shot. He's a couple of feet below where he should be."

Not my fault. The horse proved to be the culprit. He had sunk into the mud.

"Realign the camera," I urged. "For once the horse appears to be going to stand his ground."

After a time they decided I would be better if coached – not, I hasten to add, in riding, which they deemed hopeless. A carriage was produced and I dismounted from the vehicle in solitary splendour at intervals and invariably enquired, as befits the commanding officer, "Where exactly are we?"

"Marston Moor" or possibly "Paddington" I and the putative audience were informed. I then gave the order to charge, and battle commenced.

Afterwards we spent weeks in Pinewood until Harris/ Cromwell finally had his way and dethroned the King.

There was another crown involved the only other time Lew Grade entrusted me with a role. I was off in Spain then, too, that time to Malaga, where I had three roles actually: script writer, actor and director. The first morning it was raining.

I am not one to hang about and I informed the supporting cast, "You are all dismissed for the day."

I dismissed myself into the neighbouring bar and ten minutes later the sun was shining in an unclouded sky.

Treacherous place, Spain. It was my first television series and an unmitigated disaster called *If the Crown Fits.* The one it didn't fit was myself.

I still write television scripts and send them to Lew for first refusal, which is invariably forthcoming. The great thing about him is he never bears a grudge and always smokes a cigar. Once at a party I asked for £2,000 for a charity while he was relating an anecdote.

"You'll have the cheque in the morning," he told me, "don't interrupt another time."

He started the story again from the beginning. And the cheque arrived the next morning.

"We do not regard Englishmen as foreigners. We look on them only as rather mad Norwegians."

HALVARD LANGE

I had only the vaguest idea where Bergen was – Sweden or possibly Norway. Since the film was called *Song of Norway,* it must surely be the latter. It turned out to be that country's largest city and its wettest. Bergen enjoys, if that is the word, at least three and usually four times the average rainfall of any other city in Norway.

I arrived on location and was greeted by a growl.

"Not your turn," I was told.

"But surely," I protested, "I have a contract. The date is firm." In most contracts it says to report on or about a certain date, but this one was more specific.

"You'll have to talk to Mr Stone," said the assistant director. "We're still tied up with Florence Henderson." They were not, of course, literally roped together. It was just that her songs were taking longer to record than the time they had allowed.

"Yes, I do see," said Mr Stone, the director, when I flourished my contract before him. "But we shan't get to you for a week, by which time we shall be out of here." He paused, thoughtful. "Of course, all the same, it is a pity to waste the afternoon. Are you doing anything?" An idea had taken form. "Alert the crew," he informed a minion and consulting his diary he called for a phone and dialled a number.

"Mrs Eiler?" he queried. "You remember me, Richard Stone. We met at dinner once in Buenos Aires. I am on your doorstep making a picture about Edvard Grieg. You told me you live in a house he used to visit. He used to swim across the fjord to visit a sweetheart. No, that isn't in the picture so far, but one never knows. Actually I'm ringing to ask if I might come to tea. I would so like to meet you again and I have Robert Morley with me, you know the great English actor. Never mind, you'll know his face. Would it be an imposition if I were to bring him? I think it might help him with his interpretation of the part. No, he isn't actually playing Grieg. He's one of his patrons. Oh, good, I'll tell him – she liked you in *Marie Antoinette* – oh, that would be splendid. We'll come about four, shall we, or perhaps a little before? Would you mind very much if I brought a photographer? I see, you don't like having the house photographed. Quite understand. But of course he'll be concentrating on Morley. It will be fine."

The lady was not prepared for our arrival on her doorstep at about lunchtime. Nor was she prepared for the entire film crew which accompanied us. Mr Stone was his ebullient best, surveying the drawing-room and urging his followers to stop smoking and not to stamp the stubs out on the parquet.

"It is just what we wanted," he assured the bewildered hostess. "Have you, by any chance, a bed we might use?"

"Several," she told him, "but not as a rule down here."

"No trouble to move one," he assured her. "But we shall

need a large one."

Our hostess had given up.

"And we'll need a couple of brutes," he continued now completely unopposed.

The brutes, enormous arclights, were installed and a track was laid. Furniture was repositioned, pictures taken down and others rehung.

"Don't worry, it will all go back," he assured the panicking woman. "You won't notice we've been here. We'll just draw the curtains now, this is supposed to be a night scene. Pity to block out your lovely view. Grieg must have been no end of a good swimmer. How old was he at the time?"

By now the lady had a horrific vision of the dripping composer entering to damage the carpet and admitted her worry.

"Would you like us to take it up?" Stone queried.

For the first time she put her foot down firmly – on the carpet. "Certainly not," she said. "It is a fitted carpet."

Now thoroughly demoralised and bewildered, she did not remain to watch us. I climbed into the bed and struggled to remember the dialogue. After an hour or two the director appeared satisfied. Some sort of order was restored. The bed was carried back upstairs and the pictures hung back in their former positions. The track, the brutes and the crew disappeared.

"Now about the tea," he demanded.

Mr Stone was disappointed. Still, he hadn't entirely wasted the afternoon.

Mr Stone had other problems besides myself and Florence Henderson, whose return to sing at the Metropolitan in New York was impatiently awaited. Mr Harry Secombe, the well-known tenor and former Goon, was temporarily *hors de combat*, having been dislodged from a sleigh and nearly killed. Margaret Rutherford had been chucked on the first morning before a shot could be fired. There was also the director of the Norwegian National Theatre, who played Grieg and fretted at the delays. He was supposed to be organizing the new season's programme. He voiced his irritation to one of the studio's executives over on a brief visit.

"Kid," he was told, "when the picture's released you won't have to worry any more about crummy little theatre engagements."

The distinguished gentleman was still choking over the smorgasbord when I left the table.

Nothing however worried Mr Stone – that is, until the picture was finally released. Still he was used to disaster movies, having sunk the *Normandie* in a previous epic. My own involvement was certainly not a total loss. My wife and I spent a very happy week among the fjords transferring from one steamer to another and only dismissing our hired limousine, which remained on land hurrying around to greet our every disembarkation, when we discovered that the studio wasn't proposing to pay for it.

"Never any weary traveller complained that he came too soon to his journey's end."

THOMAS FULLER

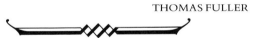

I had secured a role in what was projected to be the first of the forty episodes designed to reintroduce William Tell to small-screen viewers. With any luck, I thought, more employment would follow. I was not to play William himself, of course, but rather a wicked nobleman who had imprisoned the hapless fellow in a dungeon. A ruined castle had been selected for the action, a costume fitted and I was off to France to Chateauvillain, of which, like you, I had never heard. The first flight, to Lyons, was comparatively easy, but I missed the connecting plane. I surveyed the location on a map. I must be the poorest map reader that ever lived. Having persuaded a fellow passenger to give me a lift in what I judged to be the right direction, I finished up a hundred miles off target. As someone else was bound to be paying, I hired a taxi and arrived a good deal later. Everyone seemed to have gone to bed and I owed the driver £100. One of the first rules to be learned by an actor on location is never carry cash. There is always some official eager to advance the ready and with reasonable luck time will elapse before it has to be paid back. On very lucky occasions repayment will never be required. I had to waken the production manager before the taxi was happily driven away.

Chateauvillain is the original copper-bottomed spa. It must, I suppose, be copper or some other equally foul-tasting mineral which the patients sip by the hour. By eight the next morning I saw them promenading in the gardens below or sitting on small upright chairs waiting for the band to play and for their health to return. From my balcony I glimpsed hundreds of them in a poor state of repair clutching miniature tumblers encased in pretty wicker baskets which could be hung round the neck. I found later there wasn't to be any music from the bandstand and by ten everyone had gone to the massage parlours. Punctually at four the place filled up again and so did the patients. The hotel had a miniature spa all of its own and a supply of tumblers. It provided three separate varieties of spring water. To be on the safe side, I decided to sample them all. One sip was enough.

"What are the waters good for?" I asked the porter.

"Everything, Monsieur," he told me.

If I was to become healthy, I decided I must do it under my own steam without the aid of carbonated copper or even a pummelling.

I inspected the other hotels grouped around the valley to discover if the location manager had, as is usual, selected a superior lodging for himself, but returned satisfied. Mine was the only one apparently with a swimming-pool. I lazed in a deckchair until it was time to be fetched for the first night shooting.

A little way up the road was the ruined castle. Mr Tell was chained outside, a menacing blade swinging just above his head and liable to be lowered at any moment. I was not, I found to my satisfaction, in the first shot. Then it started to rain and we moved sort of indoors – it was not exactly indoors as the building had no roof. The casting director had selected the other players and then rather wisely decided to remain in Paris. One was a hairdresser, another up until then an unemployed fiddler, and the third simply couldn't handle the dialogue under any direction. In the end I spoke most of the lines in an attempt to convey the plot. We struggled until dawn. It was not an auspicious start to the proceedings, which did not improve noticeably over the next five days. Mr Tell, however, managed to extricate himself from the blade of Damocles and I would imagine the company managed to extricate themselves from the casting director.

There wasn't a great deal to do in Chateauvillain except to avoid the production manager, who was still anxious to retrieve his £100. I did sample the various restaurants, but found none of them outstanding. The French take their health farms seriously, unlike the British, who usually open a variety of reliable bistros within walking distance of the establishments.

The only other actor there I knew was Jeremy Lloyd, who was due to appear in the other thirty-nine episodes and was convinced his daily draught would have no lasting ill effects. There was a weight-lifter from Bermondsey, who always accompanied us in the studio car to the castle, but seldom spoke. Curious to discover his role in the proceedings, I eventually posed the question.

"I am," he informed me, "a stunt man."

"Aren't we all?" I had the wit to reply.

"At night you can't do anything because all of Belgrade is lit by a ten-watt bulb, and you can't go anywhere because Tito has the car."

MEL BROOKS

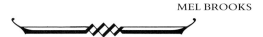

In Belgrade I played the first Caucasian Emperor of China in a film about Ghengis Khan. I hadn't intended him to be Caucasian, nor had the director, but my make-up had taken an hour and a half the first evening. Seeing that the director was shooting from a considerable distance, I told the make-up man to apply simple pancake and avoid the taping of my eyelids. Halfway through the night the rain commenced, the camera moved in and close-ups were demanded. I sensed I was in trouble. Directors of epics do not appreciate an hour's delay while the countenance of an idle actor is adjusted. I might, I told myself, get thrown off the picture before I had time to convince others of my dedication to my profession. To my rather astonished relief, no one seemed to notice. I completed my role looking much the same as usual, but with extremely long fingernails. Only on the last day, when shooting had moved to Berlin and the director invited me to take my place surrounded by genuine Chinese concubines, was any notice taken.

"I think the Emperor might stand a little apart," I suggested.

"Why aren't you made up?" he asked.

"I am," I told him. "This has been my disguise since the start of the picture." I won my point and achieved another close-up, or at least a long medium shot.

The proceedings in Belgrade were dominated by Omar Sharif, who was playing the Khan. In the script he discovered the secret of gunpowder and in no time at all, although held prisoner, he arranged to blow up the Great Wall of China.

"Why aren't you made up?" he asked

The idea was that the fuse would be lit by myself at the conclusion of a giant firework display under the impression I was igniting the final rocket. Experts arrived to stuff the wall with gelignite, but decided the evening was too damp and delayed the explosions until the next evening, when the air seemed to me much the same. Already apprehensive, we all watched a dazzling display of rockets and catherine wheels, and I marvelled that Brocks had managed to get it right – this was, after all, supposed to be the first firework display known to man. I was then handed a torch and instructed to light the fatal fuse. I suspected there was too much gunpowder. I approached overcautiously and jibbed at the crucial moment.

"Too much gunpowder, dear," I told the director, who had already given a signal for the Khan's cavalry to charge from behind. Somehow they managed to avoid me and also the wall, which remained remarkably intact. At least I had been right about the fuse. On the next evening it was lit by my double, who had his eyebrows severely singed. Just before the cameras began to turn on the devastation, one of the cast posed the question of whether or not she was in the know about the explosion which would ensue. The director invited her to adopt alternative expressions as to whether or not she knew what was to follow.

"I can't see the slightest difference," he confided reassuringly. "But, in any case, you do realize you have your back to the camera?"

I watched from a safe distance and so did he.

"Whatever happens," he instructed the cast through his megaphone, "carry on regardless. We only have sufficient gelignite for one take."

Given a few days respite by the schedule, Belgrade did not seem the place to spend them. The poetically named "white town" was at that time the drabbest of capitals. The modernish buildings were mediocre and ugly. They had risen after the most recent devastation of the city, the one carried out on Palm Sunday 1941, when 300 Nazi bombers had killed more than 25,000 people. The history of Belgrade is a history of devastation – more than twenty times it has been flattened and rebuilt because of its strategic position at the confluence of the Sava and Danube rivers. It was fortified first by the Celts. They were followed by the Romans, the Huns, the Goths, the Avars and the Turks. And now by the film unit. I decided on a trip to Sarajevo and beyond. I travelled by bus and pressed on to Budva. The journey took three full days. Fearful that I might have overstayed my leave, I rang Belgrade to apprise them of my whereabouts and was immediately informed that I was needed on the set the next morning at eight.

"Where are you?" the unit manager demanded.

"Oh, round and about," I told him. I had no qualms. Had not the guide book announced that a night express left for the capital? I approached my hotel reception desk.

"A ticket to Belgrade, please. First-class if possible and a sleeper," I added, "but I'll rough it if necessary."

"What night sleeper?" enquired the hotel porter.

"The one in the guide book," I told him and showed him the relevant page.

"Never heard of it." He looked puzzled.

"Surely you are supposed to know about trains," I scolded. "If necessary I'll go to the station and book my own ticket."

"There isn't a station," he told me.

"Why not?"

"Well, there isn't a railway. If you want to go to Belgrade you have to take a bus. It'll take three days."

"I know about that," I told him.

Yugoslavia was not yet geared up for the tourist trade, but by a lucky chance a tour leader for early pilgrims was at that moment seated in the lounge. I explained my problem.

"Taxi to Split," she advised. "From there a mail plane

leaves most evenings, but you'll have to look sharp."

We had trouble finding the airfield. On it a small plane waited. I flourished dinars and persuaded them to take a passenger. It was with a sense of shame I witnessed them emptying the plane of practically all the post. I couldn't be as heavy as that, I told myself. Seated on the very few mail bags which remained, we bumped into the night.

I arrived on location punctually – and very pleased with myself.

"You aren't needed for another three days," they said.

I sought out Michael Hordern. "We are off to the Iron Gate," I told him.

"As long as you are paying for the car," he agreed. "Anyway where is the Iron Gate and for that matter what is it?"

For some reason I had kept the perfidious guide book.

"No traveller should miss the Iron Gate," I told him. "It is a rocky and exceedingly picturesque gorge where the Danube plunges over a narrow cliff. The resulting spray is visible from a distance of ten miles."

"I'm not keen," he told me, but I hustled him into the waiting vehicle, where he promptly fell asleep.

Miles further on we passed a travelling circus, which consisted of a few gaudily painted caravans behind which, apparently unattached, trotted an enormous bear. When the entourage was behind us, safely out of sight, I woke Michael.

"Wonderful scenery," I lied, "and quite unspoiled. This is the real Yugoslavia. Why I wouldn't be surprised if we spied a bear."

He seemed impressed.

"Want to bet?" I said and named a sum I hoped would cover the cost of the dilapidated and springless taxi.

"You're on," he told me.

We waited at the side of the road until the bear caught us up. It looked as if it was unlikely to trouble us, but we thought it prudent to let it amble by while we climbed back inside the car. I don't think Michael honoured the wager. Circus bears did not count was his theory.

We saw little of the Iron Gate. The mist was impenetrable and very, very damp. I threw the guide book down into the torrent.

"We watched the ocean and the sky together
Under the roof of blue Italian weather."

PERCY BYSSHE SHELLEY

I have always perfectly understood why a man who has been happy holiday-making in Margate should choose to return August after August. For us, it was the Lido in Venice and the Hotel des Bains at the start of the Venice Film Festival. There we rented a cabana on the beach. The attendants swept the sand clear of castles during luncheon and no running about was permitted until four o'clock. There were two upright chairs, a pailful of fresh water, two deckchairs and a sunbed. No more than four occupants were allowed. Once, in the next cabana, there was a tea party for the Windsors. They came by bus from the Excelsior Hotel down the road. My wife and I were invited, but not the children. It was strange territory for us and also I imagine for the Duke, who was more often the guest of gossip columnist Elsa Maxwell. (She had two cabanas further up the row.)

If I had been asked to describe the elegant couple, which alas I never was, I might have dwelt on their manners, particularly his. He was always the first to rise and pass round the sandwiches. Snobbishness is, for me, an abiding pleasure. Once in Sunningdale my father-in-law entertained Prince Bernhard of the Netherlands, but, although I was fully grown at the time, I was not invited. It was deemed prudent that I should lunch at Ascot as I was a supporter of the Labour crowd.

If you are not a snob, you miss the enjoyable *frisson* when shaking hands with someone like the Duke of Windsor.

My wife, ever the watchful parent, once chided the head waiter of the Hotel des Bains about the lack of fresh vegetables at luncheon.

"Come early, before the rush at three," he assured her, "and you can have any you wish."

Dishes of carrots, spinach, beans appeared, only to be sternly rejected by our young.

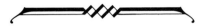

"I stood in Venice, on the Bridge of Sighs;
A palace and a prison on each hand;
I saw from out the wave her structure rise
As from the stroke of the enchanter's wand.
A thousand years their cloudy wings expand
Around me, and a dying glory smiles
O'er the far times, when many a subject land
Looked to the winged Lion's marble piles,
Where Venice sat in state, throned on her hundred isles."

LORD BYRON

Not that my brood were not appreciative of the joys of Venice. We took evening trips across the lagoon to the city, where they were forever ignoring St Mark's and brushing up on the language by translating the titles on film posters. Sheridan, always the boldest, kept demanding autographs from ladies he had previously been certain were Sophia Loren. My daughter concentrated on meticulously fashioned glass *bonbons,* always hoping that when she got home someone would be persuaded to bite.

Yet the delights of all those summer days, the beauty of the small bridges and the great picture galleries, and yes, even St Mark's Square itself, seem now rather insignificant compared to one tea-time shared with the Duchess. I cannot remember a word of the conversation, nothing of her appearance. It is just that I can add one more name to my private roll of honour, a list of the illustrious and the notorious with whom for a few years I was, so to speak, at school while we studied together some of the lessons life would teach. For my part, I have never been an apt scholar. I never learned how to listen to music or look at pictures. I only glimpsed architectural marvels and avoided, when possible, inspecting what other men had left behind in the shadows of history. I have never pondered the meaning of Stonehenge or the idols on remote islands. When I climbed Aztec steps, I was aware only of how much smaller were human feet thousands of years ago. I've met Popes and presidents, Mrs Roosevelt and Greta Garbo – and of course the Duchess. I never thought to ask them what they were up to, and what was worse, I never asked myself. I never even wondered whom I would meet next . . . in Samara or on the Blackpool Sands. But, goodness, how I enjoyed meeting them. I shall never forget the Duchess – or Venice.

"Whenever you are unhappy . . . go to Russia. Anyone who has come to understand that country will find himself content to live anywhere else."

MARQUIS DE CUSTINE

When Miss Elizabeth Taylor first arrived in Leningrad on a disastrous mission to film Maeterlinck's *Bluebird,* her first thought was to explore the security arrangements in the hotel. This was not so much for her own security, relying as we all did on the KGB for that, but for the diamonds which had been given to her by Richard Burton. The solution was to move the massive hotel safe into her equally massive suite and to hand over the keys to her impressive entourage, which included the only truly melancholic hairdresser I ever met. Hairdressers are usually the happiest of mortals, who seldom admit defeat, but this one bowed to the prevailing mood of the group who were in mourning for the absence of Mr Burton, at this time divorced from his spouse.

No one was prepared to savour the experience of the Venice of the North. Like the director, George Cukor, they were determined not to enjoy themselves. George had been on the shoot for several weeks when I arrived, and chaos prevailed. The money men, who had arrived from America, doubted if any of the picture already shot could be salvaged. The head of the Russian film industry, a powerful tycoon wearing an astrakhan collar to his overcoat, had at first railed against the extravagance and then, emerging white-faced from the projection theatre, remarked that whatever could be shown in the States, not a foot would be available to Soviet viewers. The highly skilled British editor invited to salvage the disaster declined, remarking that nothing could be achieved in the cutting process and he certainly didn't need the practice.

By the time I arrived, operations had been suspended, some of the American cast had gone AWOL, but surprisingly George was still surviving – if only just. Back home, of course, he had always relied on advisors to steer him clear of technical problems, whereas here, the technicians, jealous of "Yankee know it all", left him to flounder. In a scene in which 400 children assembled to be drilled while they waited in Maeterlinck's script to be born, quite elderly pubescent girls were divided by the authorities into two groups – one to be rehearsed in the morning and the other actually to shoot in the afternoon in order not to interrupt their schooling. I don't think anyone had bothered to tell the director, who could never understand why they had forgotten everything he had taught them before lunch as soon as the cameras began rolling.

The only persons I met who were manifestly happy were a couple from Oregon who had nothing to do with the proceedings. They had brought a quadriplegic son to the hospital, where a miraculous operation had restored him to crutches and they were now hopeful that he would soon be walking unaided. The hospital had recruited them as auxiliary nurses and the film unit as unofficial mascots.

One evening I persuaded Miss Taylor, always afraid of being mobbed, to stroll the streets.

"No one will notice," I assured her and I might have been proved correct if I hadn't chosen to take her afterwards into the hotel dining-room, where American tourists climbed on their chairs and viewed her with sharp intakes of breath, which Miss Taylor, rather paranoid at this point, interpreted as hisses.

On my last evening, with Cicely Tyson, who featured as a cat, and George Cole, who played a dog, we cruised up the Neva with some of the Italia Conti School's children and a few of the Russian children, who took over the steering while the crew sampled the hard liquor and caviar below decks.

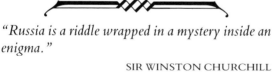

"Russia is a riddle wrapped in a mystery inside an enigma."

SIR WINSTON CHURCHILL

All arrangements were in the hands of the KGB. Unless you had these experts on foreign travel on your side, little was accomplished in Russia. As you stepped off the plane on arrival it was they who confiscated all reading matter and thrust a copy of *Time* magazine into your coat pocket, only to have it confiscated by a customs official. On the other side of the barrier the policeman waited to return your books. Later I asked one of them to explain.

"It's a sort of code," he replied. "That's why they didn't search your luggage."

"But if they weren't going to search it, why did you bother to remove my James Bond book?"

"Better always the safe side," he told me.

Unfortunately he was not at my side when I was fined for jaywalking across one of the squares. It was a not inconsiderable amount. I bet he pockets it, I told myself. In point of fact he insisted on giving me a receipt.

"A souvenir," he assured me, "of our dreaded secret police."

Once more I had misjudged the Russians. The trouble is you never quite know with them. How brilliantly they solve the problems of keeping the tourists under control – no hooray henrys for them, nor lager louts. The KGB will get you, if you don't watch out. Yet once, in Nakoda, while waiting for a slow boat to Japan, I was approached by a reckless Australian who had been trading illegally in bear skins and now had a quantity of unchangeable roubles. Unchangeable by him, at any rate. His suggestion was that I should be the one who changed them into dollars and then reimburse him once we were safely on the ship. I cringed, fearful that the Intourist guide standing nearby had heard his infamous and indeed criminal suggestion. I was right. She had.

"It's perfectly simple," she told me. "Just do as he asks."

I did and absolutely nothing happened to us, although a

travelling companion who had shared a compartment on the Trans-Siberian Railway and had persisted in snapping pictures of me on the platform as I alighted, had an exceedingly rough time. It is, it seems, strictly forbidden to photograph railway lines and supermarkets. Never ask why.

"I should like to spend the whole of my life travelling abroad, if I could anywhere borrow another life to spend afterwards at home."

WILLIAM HAZLITT

Thirty-five years ago I used to take my youngest child on holidays to the Lido. It was I who kept a watchful eye as he came down the steps and, clutching him by the hand, accepted the compliments of strangers or answered the questions of passersby. Now he takes my arm and, because I discard my hearing aid for fear of endangering it in the pool, assures others that I was never, in fact, in *The Hunchback of Notre Dame,* and makes sure that no one pats me on the head. It was he who reassured me about the flight delay during the high season at Gatwick, which in truth turned out to be less than an hour, and he also who convinced me of the beauty of extremely low fares on package tours to Malta.

I had a very nice balcony at the Dragonara Palace Hotel, which is no longer operated by Ladbrokes, but still has a superb restaurant and a casino. My son plays roulette almost as badly as I do and at the table the age factor seemed to disappear for a time as well as the money. He stayed with a friend who took us on a wild goose chase to view the now abandoned airfield where he served in the Navy during the war and to the hospital where he left his tonsils. The excursions ended usually in Medina, wonderfully walled and fortified by the crusaders and the site of a couple of splendid restaurants, whose names I have of course forgotten.

The doctor who briefly attended me when I feared a recurrence of an old leg inflammation reassured me, while prescribing an excellent new ointment. He recommended what he claimed was the best food in Malta. The restaurant was situated in a remote village. The food was not actually the best, but the establishment, it turned out, was owned by his cousin. This is not an uncommon occurrence, since most of the local residents tend to be related. They are a closely knit community, but all seemed extremely friendly and patient with the tourists.

In the evenings a small battalion of lager louts tends to concentrate on Pub City just over the brow of the hill, opposite the hotel. They seem to claim equal rights on the road with the motorists and to resent bitterly the sound of a car horn.

The traffic in the daytime is equally chaotic and there is a delightful absence of wardens or traffic cops. It is rather too hot for a stroll and, whenever I took one, it was invariably in the wrong direction, but cars always stopped after a while and I was frequently given a lift by a friendly native back to the open-air theatre where Verdi's *Otello* was being performed by the National Opera of Poland. It was not very good and I beat a hasty retreat, although I was faced with an hour's walk in search of food. I was desperately contemplating a Wimpy bar when I was accosted by an English couple, who enquired what had brought me to such an outlandish hole. They were the exception to the rule, as they found no fun in Malta and couldn't imagine why they had been lured on such a disastrous holiday. They did, however, recommend a most satisfactory restaurant a few yards further along the very street I was on.

Once, deciding to walk by the docks which still bear the traces of ferocious war damage, I despaired of finding a cool hideaway and a gin and tonic until I came across a sort of abandoned cave, presided over by a proprietor who played a never-ending game of patience and his assistant who had never heard of gin or tonic. He recommended a glass of Ecstasy, a milky substance flavoured with vanilla – a strong local favourite. On the wall was an enormous poster of Manchester United football team, so perhaps the cave did better business in the evenings. I suppose I was as near to the true Malta there as I was ever likely to be. They seemed a drowsy, contented lot, no more disturbed by package tours than they had been by Napoleon, Nelson or Mintoff, nor for that matter by the Knights.

"Paris is a veritable ocean. Take as many soundings in it as you will, you will never know its depth."

HONORÉ DE BALZAC

I am not one to overpraise the French. As Noël Coward discovered when he was appearing at the Comédie Française, they don't seem to understand their own language. Grasping the door of the taxi and attempting to instruct the driver on one's destination leads to periods of frustration. *"Je désire la place du Pyramid, Monsieur,"* seems only to nonplus.

I don't think there is really much wrong with my accent acquired in my very early years at Westgate-on-Sea. Certainly my elder son, who has spent years abroad and is a master of the tongue, having taken great pains to acquire even the Gallic shrug when he addresses the natives, usually has to conclude by ordering his meal in English.

The French, of course, are born torturers. I once watched from fifty yards away in the Rue St Honoré (the one with the pillars) while one of them lifted a fellow countryman almost tenderly and proceeded to use him as a battering ram; finally he deposited the apparent corpse on the pavement outside a café and he went inside, presumably in search of the customary *fin* decreed for his behaviour.

I abandoned my usual caution and went in pursuit, demanding a telephone to summon a gendarme.

"*Salaud*," I shouted at the customers. "*Quoi*," I demanded, "would de Gaulle *pensait de vous?*"

It was some time ago. I never discovered the General's reaction as, during my efforts to contact the constabulary, the corpse rose, apparently unscathed and walked briskly away. At least I refused the proprietor's demand that I should pay for the call.

"*C'était un neuf, neuf, neuf,*" I told him.

They are a hard-headed lot, the French.

Nor do I care very much for the condescension of the head waiters in the more expensive eateries. Once, in Montmartre, I had the heady delight of being served a bottle of wine which was corked. Never before and never since in my life had this happened to me. The waiter responded to my beckoning call, nose in the air, but was almost humbled when he was encouraged to bring said nose into proximity with the wine. I could not have enjoyed it more. He did not of course, apologise, but I sensed almost respect in his attitude.

There was no such redress with the ladies who man the lavatories. There was always a replied rebuke in their attitude.

"You are a fool to pay such prices," I could always hear them thinking. "You should attend to these matters before you come out."

Paris remains the great barrier to travel in Europe. "You will have to go through Paris," the travel agent informs. This is not as easy as he supposes.

De Gaulle, an aptly named airport if there ever was one, is a forbidding adventure. And then there is Le Bourget. These are two airports uneasily separated by courtesy buses and one is usually *mal placé*.

French railway stations are simpler and I suppose it must be admitted far cleaner than our own. They are also, of course, abnormally empty. The French seldom run trains. The average *gare,* in the country at least, seems to accommodate at the most, four or five trains a day. French travellers tend to make a special journey to the station some time before the intended date of departure. They are not natural spenders and, having parted with the ready, usually require a period to recover and recuperate from the extravagance.

The Pullman, the *wagon-lit* are things of the past. No longer are there four courses served at individual tables lit by pink-shaded lamps. Horrendous sandwiches are now poked through windows from platform trolleys or handed out by uniformed attendants. Cellophane takes the place of butter. The contents (either salami or cheese) are as dry as the bread. Never ask for whom the bell tolls when the trolley makes its appearance; certainly it no longer tolls for the *premier service.*

In the station buffets they serve the inevitable steak and chips in surroundings as tough as the meat itself. Everything is disposable, from the paper napkins wrapped round the disposable plastic contents, including the disposable spoon to stir the coffee. It is no longer even a spoon, but a small two-pronged fork. One day soon there will be enlarged litter bins to accommodate previous customers, also disposable.

"France was long a despotism tempered by epigrams."
THOMAS CARLYLE

Sooner or, hopefully, later the Channel tunnel (the target of the underground terrorist) will be completed. No longer will we be able to sample the fresh air of Folkestone before embarkation to Le Touquet, where, I must admit, I spent a very happy sixtieth birthday. On the northern coast there is almost too much sand, too many dunes to be negotiated, but the memory of my birthday persists. The whole family went on two chartered planes and the French had thoughtfully proclaimed it a day of rejoicing with a strike of customs officers. Our progress was unimpeded by French officialdom. There were no formalities to detain us on our way to lunch at Flavio's and giant meringues. After lunch, Gladys Cooper terrified the natives as she drove a go-kart through the streets. In her unskilled hands it turned into a formidable juggernaut. There were endless group photographs under a Renoir sky and then it was off to the Casino au Fôret, where even the grandchildren were allowed to watch the *boule*. The villas of the place echo triumphs at the baccarat table – "Banco" and "Suivi" they are called. Here, too, is a reminder of a personal disaster. Once in my salad days I was sharing the bank and I misunderstood the instruction of the croupier and drew on a seven. I retreated in shame from the outrage, acrimony and cries of *"faux tirage"*.

I never again touched a playing card in France. Perversely, they omit to number them.

The handlers of horses reluctant to enter the stall are supplied with lists identifying their charges. Casino authorities keep a similar check on players applying for re-admission. At least, I have never had to be blindfolded, but have I, I wonder, earned the notation *"maladroit"*? The phrase can also mean *gauche,* which is why, I suppose, the French have bequeathed both to us, having no further use for the terms themselves. The French have always placed too great an importance on style.

3
Down Under

Clinging to home, with my own daughter Annabel in
Outcast of the Islands

3
DOWN UNDER

"And all lying mysteriously within the Australian underdark, that peculiar lost weary aloofness of Australia. There was the vast town of Sydney. And it didn't seem to be real, it seemed to be sprinkled on the surface of a darkness into which it never penetrated."

D. H. LAWRENCE

I F YOU ASK me, and, since no one has, I shall ask myself, what has changed the cities I used to visit in more spacious times from regular motion into chronic constipation? It is, of course, the motorcar. Morning and evening it bedevils the anxious commuter. Will he arrive on time at his place of work? Almost certainly not. Where is he to park his offending transport? Citizens demand to be elsewhere and are obliged to remain stationary in traffic jams of their own making.

How different was Sydney when I was there just after the war. There were other problems, of course, but you could still cruise in comparatively empty streets. Indeed, if you took a taxi, you were obliged to do so. It was the rule with the driver to proceed in the opposite direction to your destination in search of others to fill up his cab.

Bars and licensed restaurants served no drink after 6 p.m. Bottles of wine were placed discreetly under the table or risked being impounded by the ever watchful and thirsty local constabulary. Illegal gambling joints were transformed momentarily into bridge clubs by the entrance of one or more customers wearing mackintoshes. The bars filled at 5 p.m. and emptied an hour later. The schooners carefully stacked on the counters, the customers less tenderly laid out on the grass verges to recover in their own good time. You stepped warily through the stage door, if, like me, you had taken a play to the land of Oz. Theatre tickets could not be bought at the box-office. If you wanted to buy one, you would first have to go to the local pharmacist. The Taits, who ran the theatre and the chemist, were deaf to all complaints. It would be dangerous, they assured me, to keep valuable seats in row E within easy reach of a smash-and-grab raider.

On the first night of *Edward, My Son* the cast struggled with the stage crew. Moving to Melbourne a few weeks later, I announced the first performance would be reserved for the blind who would, if they were fortunate, hear something of the piece and not see a single scene shifter. Never at any time was I popular with the management.

Then, as now, one feels safe in Sydney. True, nowadays there is still the threat of the occasional mugger, the menacing surfboard, but it is in the outback that the real dangers lurk – trapdoor spiders, rattle snakes, high-kicking kangaroos, munchies who lurk just off shore and jellyfish floating off Bondi beach to wrap their tentacles around your testicles and occasionally sting you to death. There was never a land where the people were so friendly and the fauna so inimical. What fascinating people they were: the bookmaker who on the first Friday of the month lived in terror of his butler, who returned on that day from the post office from whence he had dispatched his wife's alimony payment and in a drunken rage assaulted his employer. One day the lady died and, having nothing to do on the following monthly atonement day, the butler took to his bed and died himself. There was the last of the Kidmores, who, removed from Cheltenham

Ladies College at the age of twelve, tracked with her father from Adelaide to Brisbane, always remaining within their vast home pastures, with a herd of aborigine cattlemen who refused to make the journey without knowledge of the next waterhole. There were a few families of enormous wealth who had it made and a multitude of wingeing Poms who hadn't. "This one", old Mr Fairfax remarked to me, indicating has grandson aged eight, "will one day be the cleverest of us all." It was a proud prophecy which now seems unlikely to be fulfilled: the boy grew up to dismember the empire and sell the *Sydney Morning Herald*.

"Welcome to modern day Tahiti! That's just what it is – noise. Hundreds of motorcycles, motorbikes, Vespas trailbikes, automobiles and trucks all zoom along zigzagging in and out of traffic trying to get there first . . . Look out on the lagoon and there is more noise. Even the traditional outrigger canoes have engines on them."

JAN PRINCE

The idea seemed sound, at least in theory. Assemble an international cast preferably one from each country, and shoot ahead. Belmondo came from France; Ursula Andress came from Hollywood. Leading players were summoned from Turkey, Italy, Greece and Russia. I travelled from England. We spoke in French or tried to, but, whenever I gave Belmondo his carefully rehearsed cue, he dissolved into helpless laughter.

A determined explorer, I arrived in Tahiti a week early and, having inspected the Gauguin Museum, which contained no examples of the great artist's work but only his discarded palette and photographs of his studio hut, I cooled my heels in the hotel pool in the company of the only other residents –

an unsuccessful fire-eater, who practised assiduously and suffered from a badly burnt tongue, and his current girl friend, who also rehearsed daily, stepping into a small black box, which for the fire-eater served as an encore as he skewered it with knives and she emerged scratched and bleeding.

"She'll never learn," he confided. "The girl's an idiot."

The unfortunate couple were stranded and scanned the ocean anxiously for the sight of a cruise ship on which they hoped to embark as cabaret artistes. He had vague hopes of insinuating himself into the film script.

"From what you tell me," he said, "there should surely be a place for someone from Dublin."

The producer, when he did arrive, had planned to shoot in Bora-Bora, but abandoned the plan, it was said, because he was fearful of encountering his ex-wife who was currently suing him for alimony. Instead he made the disastrous choice of an alternative island a good few kilometres from base, whither we proceeded in the early morning by bus, completing the journey by outrigger canoes. No one had told him that the rain came punctually at three in the afternoon or that the island was inhabited by ferocious tree-climbing crabs which were wont to sever the cables and only occasionally to electrocute themselves. I suppose that didn't matter as much as the fact that, when shooting had to be abandoned, we were obliged to climb back into the canoes now filled with water. When caught in a shower, the residents merely removed their top clothing and proceeded in their underwear, but the wardrobe department was adamant that we should not follow their example.

"We have enough work drying out the costumes as it is," they protested. In point of fact nothing ever quite dries in Tahiti.

With pneumonia imminent, a fresh crisis occurred. No one was being paid. Intercontinental telephone lines were jammed each evening by the cast connecting with their agents in Europe. For some reason it was impossible to phone London. Eventually proceedings were halted and resumed in Nice, or, at any rate, just off it, on a yacht cruising off the Côte d'Azur. I left Belmondo still chuckling, but I imagine he stopped laughing when the disastrous film was eventually released.

Years later I went back to Tahiti; I made a pilgrimage to the hotel, but there was no trace of the fire-eater. How unfair life is to be sure. Some are born with a silver spoon in their mouth; others with a petrol torch.

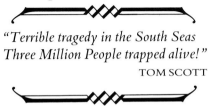

"Terrible tragedy in the South Seas
Three Million People trapped alive!"
TOM SCOTT

Stage actors travelling the world are apt to prefer cities where they play to full houses, which is why, at the other end of the spectrum, I have never really been fond of Glasgow or Auckland. I don't say people actually go to New Zealand to escape me, but, when I do visit, I am usually disappointed in the 'take'. Small wonder that for my part I find New Zealanders dull: they are the only people in the world who stay awake counting sheep.

On my first visit a large wave tipped me out of bed at the entrance to the harbour. Water flooded the cabin. The captain, or more probably the pilot, was as surprised as I was.

"I cannot imagine what it was doing there," he remarked later. "Most unusual."

Nothing went right after that. Incautiously, I insulted the whitebait. Almost as soon as we docked they were spooned into my mouth on television and I spat them out. Normally I am fond of the little fishes, deep fried, in batter that is. These were moist and soggy and grublike in texture. Anzacs are slow to anger and also to forgive. After my stage performance complete strangers came round complaining, not about my acting, on which they seldom remarked, but to berate me for despising their national dish. Worse was to follow. At a press conference they covered the tables with mud crabs. At least I wasn't expected to eat them, but they seemed prepared to feast on me.

With some days to spare before opening night we inspected the glow-worms of Waitoma, gliding through the dark caverns silently. "Positively no smoking," the boatman warned. At the flicker of a match or the glow from a cigarette the creatures extinguish themselves.

Then there were performing sheep to watch. Their repertoire was not extensive. At the sound of their breed bleating through a loudspeaker, they appeared on the stage and afterwards just stood there in groups of three. I had expected more. A dance perhaps – or counting. True their fleeces were spick and span, and the head ram had a beard and ferocious horns.

On the way to South Island – a foolhardy expedition crossing the Timor Sea in a single-engine plane, forced to split up the family and dreading engine failure – we stopped at the mud flats, pools of deep bubbling slime in which you can disappear in ten seconds. In Christchurch we inspected glaciers and a famous bar where South Pole explorers traditionally ordered gin and tonic with ice before setting out for the real thing and perishing from frost bite and blizzards. Their last photographs were displayed on the walls.

An old Hungarian introduced me to his three sons.

"That's all you need," he confided. "One to grow the grapes, another to make the wine."

"And the third?" I prompted.

"To sell the stuff. You don't need daughters, but you do

need a wife, of course. You send for her from Budapest once you have her photograph."

He seemed reasonably content and very prosperous.

We prospected for flakes of gold armed with what my daughter called "aspiring" bottles. A genuine prospector led us to a mountain stream and I tried to persuade him to spend an evening in the theatre.

"Too busy," he excused himself.

"Afraid you might miss a nugget?" I chided.

"Growing tomatoes," he explained.

If there was gold in the hills, we never found it and, I suspect, nor did he.

In the hotel they served a Victorian dinner at six. There were seven courses and it was a rush to get to the stage door. They even offered a sorbet half way through. It was the first time I encountered the custom and long before British restaurant proprietors adopted the habit of serving frozen cointreaus to sharpen the taste buds – or perhaps to freeze them.

"No man will be a sailor who has contrivance enough to get himself into jail; for being in a ship is being in a jail, with the chance of getting drowned."

SAMUEL JOHNSON

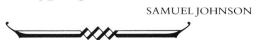

"I would like," I informed the Sydney booking clerk in the offices of P & O, "to sail home as soon as possible on one of your more comfortable ships. We are a party of five, including two children and their nurse, and I would like three cabins, though we could possibly manage with two and a stateroom. I must emphasize the word comfortable, otherwise I shall fly."

"I strongly advise you to do so then," he replied. "We have

absolutely no accommodation available on any of our sailings until early next spring."

By this time I had decided on a life on the ocean wave and was not to be deterred. "I imagine you have cancellations," I said.

"Not often. But I'll put your name on the waiting list if you wish. I must warn you it is a long one."

I wrote my telephone number down and gave it to the telephonist wrapped round a twenty dollar bill. "Ring me as soon as you hear of a cancellation," I cajoled her, and eventually she did, which is why we found ourselves a few weeks later installed in two small cabins on the port side of a ship. Port is supposed to be the preferred side on the outward journey from England. Starboard returning – hence the word POSH. We were to retain only one cabin after Bombay, but something was sure to turn up – at least I supposed it was. In point of fact it didn't, but at least the children and nurse could stay put, while my wife and I caught a plane. The last glimpse I had of the children was at bathtime when Lysol was diluted with the water as we had all been ashore through the Gates of India.

These were disciplined days and the Captain and Purser were constantly inspecting our quarters. We dressed for dinner and folded our clothes at all times.

A few days in Bombay and we were off to Cairo, confident that we would be home in time to welcome our loved ones. In Cairo we met up with Mr Abdullah, who was not only a personal friend of King Farouk but also our guide to the Pyramids, the treasure of Tutankhamun and an extraordinary number of sarcophagi of the earlier ancestors of his chum. We had to miss out the belly dancers as at 5 p.m. precisely he absented himself to play bridge, poker or any of the other diversions his patron demanded. At noon he waited on us in surprisingly good health for one who on his own admission had been up most of the night.

"Would you like to meet the King?" he asked.

"Very much," I told him. "From all accounts he sounds a particularly merry monarch."

Alas the audience never materialized, but the memory of the treasures in the Cairo museum has always lingered and particularly the golden death mask.

On we went to Rome, where, still feeling disappointed by our failure to meet King Farouk, I insisted that a friend organize an audience with the Pope. Luckily that was accomplished, as one failure in the Grand Tour was sufficient as far as I was concerned.

One of the more irritating phenomena of travel is that, having taken the trouble to view the wonders of the world *in situ*, they almost all turn up in London: the golden mask at the Royal Academy, terracotta warriors at Selfridge's and even the Pope eventually in his Popemobile. At least the Sydney Opera House has had the grace to stay put.

"Whenever I look at a mountain I always expect it to turn into a volcano."

ITALO SVEVO

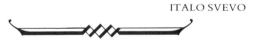

The volcano on Hawaii had been extinct for nearly a million years. Led by the warden, we approached cautiously. One never knows.

"What would you do," one of the party demanded, "if it should start up again?"

"Stop it, Madam."

I was glad it was not I who had asked.

Earlier we had lost Mother-in-law on the slopes. She was found deep in conversation with an elderly Chinese lady.

"I never knew you spoke Chinese," I said.

"I don't."

"Then how did you manage?"

"We are both grandmothers," she replied.

I have never been disappointed in Hawaii, even when making a picture there. We spent a few days tied up in harbour pretending to be at sea. Make-believe Japanese dive bombers pretended to tear holes in my waistcoat. Waikiki beach was all pretence. Skyscrapers, pretending to be condominiums, lined up on the beach to be photographed. There were tourists pretending to be parachutists and children pretending to be surf riders. Far out the veterans pretended to master the waves. There I was once photographed suspended by my ankles pretending to be a sailfish, while the actual fish, grasping my rod, pretended to be the angler. Once I pretended to be a prince and stayed at the Halekalani Hotel with the family, assuming that someone else would be paying. I found that too was pretence. Not that I grudged the expense. The elevators alone were worth the money.

Off Maui the whales returned with their offspring from the breeding grounds borne by the Humboldt currents which are thoughtfully provided by nature. They were viewed through binoculars thoughtfully provided by the Japanese.

On our first visit years earlier we found Hawaii more or less devoid of tourists. A strike of the Matson Line, which in those days ferried passengers from the mainland, and infrequent flights before the age of jet travel ensured that we had the place more or less to ourselves. We lived at an exquisite small hotel, the Coral Strand, and bathed from the reef. The rain over Diamond Head came punctually at four every afternoon and, seldom lasting more than an hour, ensured the hibiscus stayed in bloom and could be fashioned into *leis*. Everyone garlanded themselves with one at least.

We island-hopped to Lanai, where the fountains sprayed pineapple juice. American residents boasted of remote

Hawaiian ancestors. Maui, in its turn, boasted of the Hana ranch on what was then the fashionable side of the island adjacent to the rain forests and there were helicopter tours of the homes of the legendary movie stars glimpsed through the clouds. There were vast pastures of grazing cattle.

The propellors of the SS *Aorangi*, on which we voyaged to Australia, are still preserved in the Hawaiian Marine Museum. Even then the ship was something of a museum piece. My wife, the gentlest of her sex, only shows her mettle where the cubs are involved. Ours had originally been allotted cribs, but were long since past the age when they could be expected to curl up in them.

"Send for the Captain," she demanded.

"Don't you mean the Purser?" I suggested. "You can't send for the Captain. If there is trouble, he sends for you."

But the harassed gentleman appeared to sort out the accommodation. Later on the voyage I noticed he usually approached the rails with his eyes shut.

"I can't bear to estimate our speed," he informed me. "We can have speed or we can have air-conditioning, but not both. And the passengers will demand air-conditioning."

The old ship may not have been the *Mauretania* or the *Queen Mary*, setting records racing each other, but it was peaceful. As we drifted across the Pacific Ocean my heart warmed to the Captain and his crew. How nice that even the anchor is now a museum piece.

4
The New World

Oscar Wilde took his genius to America; I followed some years later

4
THE
NEW WORLD

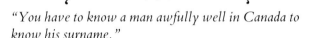

"You have to know a man awfully well in Canada to know his surname."

JOHN BUCHAN

NOBODY TOLD me that this was the day or possibly the week when they stopped the Niagara Falls or at least reduced the cascade to a mere trickle. It was a disappointment akin to my viewing the sunrise at Ayer's Rock when the gloomy edifice was reputed to turn pink, only at the base mind you.

"Wrong time of year," they told me. "You should try again in September."

I tried again the same evening. There wasn't even a dingo in sight. There was a good deal more to see in Niagara when the Falls disappointed – fun palaces, hamburger joints, souvenir shops and advertised trips under the Falls with complimentary mackintoshes.

"The rocks are being repaired," they pointed out.

This might, I thought, have been a good day to try the barrel approach, but I hadn't brought one with me. There were postcards commemorating the late Mr Blondin and reprinted newspapers recording the adventurous deed, and a baby who had survived his unique adventure holiday. As on motorways at home, I could see no workmen repairing the surface, but at least there was an absence of traffic cones as well as an absence of water.

I decided to try a journey across the Rockies. The Canadian Pacific Railway advertised a trip from Vancouver. I flew there and searched the bookshops for a copy of *The Spike*, a thrilling account of the building of the railway line, or so I had been informed. It seemed the volume was out of print, but I was offered a copy of *Larger than Life*, a life of myself written by my daughter-in-law.

"This is sure to interest you," he told me.

So it had, once.

The train left as dusk was falling. After two hours trundling cautiously through the suburbs there was no moon to light the miles of deserted track. In the restaurant car I shared a table with a lady executive who confided she was a regular passenger.

"I come here for peace and quiet," she said, "certainly not for the food, which, as you have no doubt observed, is pretty terrible."

Most of the other customers were in uniform. The train, it appeared, carried a large crew.

I determined to retire early and wake at six to make my way to the observation coach. It was still pitch black at eight. Finally, at first light, the snow appeared. There were enormous drifts on either side. A few fir trees and the occasional signal box provided the only excitement. In one of them I thought I saw a bear officiating at the levers. Panic set in. What if a tree fell, or the noise of the train precipitated an avalanche? Was this why we went so slowly? What would happen if we did break down? In the restaurant car the band was playing. It wasn't a live band, but they had mended the public address system. The crew were finishing a hearty breakfast. This is what it must have been like on the *Titanic*, I thought. I laced my coffee with brandy. The music stopped. This is it, I thought. But the voice from the bridge announced not disaster but our imminent arrival in Banff. Passengers were instructed to have their hand luggage and skis ready to disembark. A motley band of Yetis left the station. It was still snowing. The train pulled out and eventually we left the danger behind and arrived at the edge of prairie country – Calgary, where the Duke of Windsor had once bought a ranch. I disembarked there and went in search, not of cattle, but of an airport.

Montreal seemed to be a different country.

"The Queen would not dare to get out of her car here," they told me.

No one disputes that the French can cook. In Montreal they stew the moose, boil the bears and sauce the reindeer. At the Château Fontenac they serve afternoon tea to the sounds of a string orchestra wearing pigtailed powdered wigs. I was allotted a stifling room in the crow's nest. The Château is ostensibly a liner aground on the rocks. Struggling with the radiator, it seemed impossible to dampen down the boiler. In the middle of the night I changed cabins. Morning came and still no one had managed to refloat the vessel.

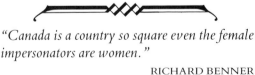

"Canada is a country so square even the female impersonators are women."

RICHARD BENNER

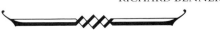

Incongruous is the word for Canada, but no one had prepared me for Honest Ed Mirvish, to whose theatre in Toronto I entrusted the world première of a piece I had written about transvestite members of the Garrick Club. I was growing accustomed to throwing my weight around and declined to attend the dress rehearsal on the grounds that the dressing-rooms were inadequately furnished. I demanded armchairs, carpets, uncracked mirrors and sufficient lighting.

Ed informed me that all would be in order by late afternoon. I agreed to rehearse and he was as good as his word. I didn't know he owned practically all the adjacent property including restaurants, shopping arcades and a furniture shop. He had even foreseen that no one was likely to care much for the piece I was performing and managed to sell all the tickets in advance of opening. We played to packed houses of chauffeurs, domestic staff and members of the nursing profession as, having seen the notices, the original purchasers of the tickets disposed of them.

Canada is a land of milkshakes and maple syrup. When the leaves turn golden and the tree trunks are tapped, the natives explore the vast igloos of shopping shelters and listen to hourly reports of the outdoor temperature and take heed lest they freeze to death on the pavements. In Beijing they bicycle to keep warm, but in Toronto they send their Cadillacs in advance to meet them in Miami.

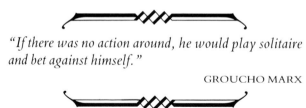

"If there was no action around, he would play solitaire and bet against himself."

GROUCHO MARX

In my book, and this after all is one, Atlantic City is strictly paste compared to the genuine sparkle of Las Vegas. It does have the advantage, however, of being considerably easier to reach from these shores, being only a three- or four-hour bus ride from the midtown Port of New York Authority on Forty-Sixth Street. It is the only ride I know where the fare is refunded on arrival. A short distance from the city the vehicle comes to a stop and officials board, not to inspect travel documents but to hand back to travellers the amount they have paid for their tickets in the form of vouchers entitling them to further free rides on the gambling tables and a complimentary swing on the giant jackpots. Thus reimbursed, it is possible to go further and win a fortune. The only discipline required is that you must rejoin your carrier precisely five hours after it has set you down. Five hours is considered the right space of time in which to lose your money and afterwards enjoy the boardwalk with its pitiful array of cheap souvenir shops, and salt water taffy, and, if in an adventurous mood, patronize a tattoo parlour and emerge with a snake up your bottom. It is not usually as sunny as Vegas and not nearly so warm. A brief stroll in Atlantic gales and you become something of a sandman. The pier, now totally enclosed, contains an enormous shopping arcade and every example of delicious fast foods from Belgian strawberry waffles through spare ribs, inspired ice-cream mixtures to Indonesian satays. Why no one has ever realized pier potential in Britain remains a mystery to me – as does the hinterland behind the casinos in Atlantic City. The slums are horrendous. Houses are boarded up or summarily burnt to the ground. When you see the graffiti, the squatters, the skeletons of abandoned cars and vandalized phone booths, you might be in Harlem – or even nearer home. The slums remain a perpetual reproach to the city fathers who believed a gambling licence was the panacea to bring prosperity.

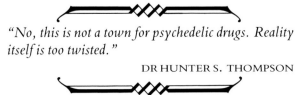

"No, this is not a town for psychedelic drugs. Reality itself is too twisted."

DR HUNTER S. THOMPSON

In time I got tired of Blackpool but never of Las Vegas, a town which should have been twinned with it. When I first found it, it was just a couple of casinos at the crossroads. The players were miners who retained their steel helmets and silver dollars. Now it is bedlam and I love it. The airport has a unique public address system voiced by the stars who warn you to take care stepping off the escalators. Afterwards care is thrown to the winds. I can never afford to stay as long as I would wish. Once I even borrowed from the pit bosses themselves in an effort to prolong my stay. When I arrived home to my mother-in-law, Gladys Cooper, in Los Angeles with whom I was staying, I urged her to send them a cheque.

"They'll be round with knuckle dusters," I warned her. "They'll take my shoes and socks and dump me in the desert."

She laughed at my fears, but I suppose she sent the money eventually. I never tried borrowing again. One last swing of the giant jackpot and I am off to settle my hotel bill with my American Express card, and to search for the other half of the air ticket.

I once took Gladys to Vegas. Having no reservation, I announced my name clearly to the desk clerk and informed him of a previous booking made by my secretary. The fellow inspected his file in vain.

"I don't know what you are talking about," Gladys interposed. "You know quite well you haven't a secretary and, if they haven't two rooms, I spotted a very nice little motel up the road with a swimming-pool."

But when we arrived at the latter we were informed no bathing was permitted after six and in no time at all we were back at Caesar's Palace eating humble pie. Not all that humble as it turned out, as we were subsequently conducted to the last available penthouse suite with a daily rate of alarming proportions.

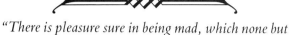

"There is pleasure sure in being mad, which none but madmen know."

DRYDEN

I prefer to visit alone. In Vegas you wake when you wake. There is no way without a watch you can tell the time. As you pull the curtains there is the desert and usually the sunshine, and in the distance the mountains which encircle the sand. It is a gigantic bunker and, unless you have filled in the questionnaire the night before, no way of getting coffee and toast. It seems simple enough to pick up the phone and order two eggs, sunny side up, rolls and grits, but you then have to practise an hour or so's meditation waiting for its arrival. And then, when it finally does appear, there is almost certainly an absence of some essential. You may have forgotten to order hot milk or someone else has forgotten to provide a knife or a spoon for the jam, in any case you can't unscrew its lid unless you hold it under the hot water tap or stick it in the door hinge. It is better to don linen slacks and a tee-shirt and venture in the elevator. There are banks of these, but it is not easy to know which one is on the way down. Miss a couple and then a hit, and a hurried sortie lest the doors close on the tardy bottom. Elevators don't like to be kept waiting unlike the patrons queuing interminably for the Garden Lounge, where you are bidden to wait for the hostess to serve you, unless, like me, you despair of ever encountering her and wander off to the casino proper to find even at that early morning hour a few tables open and bleary-eyed croupiers still spinning the ivory balls. They have been there for a good deal of the night and I shall be here for the rest of the day. I meant, of course, to try one of the pools or the sunshine on a daybed or at least to try and master the jacuzzi plumbing in my bathroom.

I haven't even shaved and now its nearly twelve, and I am still trying to find the number. The right one that is, among thirty-six and two zeros. It's not impossible to win as long as you don't play too long, but then, of course, there is nothing else to do. I don't like watching the others.

There was a lady one morning with silver minks and hair

to whom the croupiers appeared unusually deferential, even reserving her own white coloured chips. She disputed almost invariably the exact location of her stake, claiming an *en plein* when only entitled to *à cheval*. She played almost as long hours as I did and, when she left and cashed in the chips, the croupier set them aside for her probable return.

"You certainly treat the old girl like a princess," I observed.

"She is a princess," I was told. "She owns the joint ever since her husband died."

To own a casino, to play roulette all day – surely the ultimate merry widowhood.

At one I quit and returned to the cafeteria. By now it is buffet style with no hope of corned beef hash and apple pie *à la mode*, my staple (and, alas, these days as far as the hash is concerned) and unfashionable diet. The spread is enormous, but the plates economical in size.

Soon I am back in my bedroom. Why bother to shave? It is better to try and remember where I hid my stack of dollars. I search my underpants. I empty my socks. Then I suddenly remember the dollars are downstairs in the safe deposit box. I find the key concealed in the box containing my hearing aid. This time the elevator is mysteriously waiting to take me downstairs. I press the button and am admitted through the secret door. All I have to do now is to tell the attendant the maiden name of my deceased grandmother in order to open the box and give myself the money – or at least some of it.

Where to next, I ask myself. The Tropicana? The Sands? The Dunes? The Desert Inn? It was there I once hoped that an exclusive interview with Howard Hughes, who lived on the floors above, might solve my temporary cash-flow problem. But I was to be disappointed. The Circus was at least within walking distance or would have been if it were cooler, but the swinging trapeze artists overhead might distract me or even break through the net and crash, scattering my pile of chips. It would be better to take a taxicab downtown, where the casinos were not separated by distances insisted on by the drivers on the strip, but jostle each other in the main street. The Freemont, the Golden Horseshoe, the Silver Nugget, the Magic Carpet and so on and so on. Just time perhaps to munch a hamburger on rye amid the exhausted poker players who look as if they've been up all night and, in fact, have been. They are not all tourists by any means downtown. Some are residents who have become ensnared like insects in orchid traps existing God knows how and God knows on what, snatching sleep or someone's handbag, spinning the tale panhandling. Wasted veterans live to fight again briefly at the crap table. I, who don't play craps and am not yet in a wheelchair, am oddly comforted by the plight and the courage of others.

Downtown the minimum stakes are lower and I can play in quarters – even dimes at some tables. The money lasts longer; sometimes till late afternoon. The noise of the slots are the waves breaking on the shore. Now and again the bells ring and cascades of dimes hurtle into the trays beneath to be scooped into paper cups.

No one expects to win in the long run, which perpetually puzzles the unaddicted.

"Why do it then?" they ask.

"Because I love it," I reply.

"You must be mad," they say.

"It's only temporary," I assure them. "Soon I shall be up and away, but not while the dollars last."

It is only 6 p.m. and I must hurry back to the hotel to replenish and count what remains. I suppose I must have a bath sometime and certainly a shave. I turn the pages of the Vegas *Times* to see who is in town. The entertainers are mostly figures from my own youth. Liberace is dead, but not Sinatra, Tom Jones, Harry Belafonte. There was a time when such headliners were comparatively free, but now the show is more expensive and is preceded by a horrific dinner menu. Do I really want to see George Burns and his cigar again? I decide on a gourmet dinner instead, pay by card and keep my dollars intact until later. The food peaks in the evening. Up market there are a number of choices. You can eat Hawaiian, Indian, Chinese, Japanese, Spanish, Roman or steak house. I take my time. I have even shaved and put on a suit. I pose as the great food critic, after all I once was one. I feast and muse on which numbers are most likely to come up later. I haven't seen a fifteen all day. In the casino a long queue snakes round the tables seeking admittance to the late show. No dinner there, but three complimentary drinks and Bill Cosby. I caught his act once. He talked about his daughter and her panic over her first menstruation. It is surprising what the audience will listen to when you are a star.

I watch the high rollers round the crap table. The table bosses too come from a different generation. This is what they used to look like in the days of George Raft. I find a seat at the roulette wheel and begin my quest for fifteen. By four o'clock in the morning all the money is gone. Another half an hour and my luck would definitely have turned. Desperate remedies suggest themselves. Should I approach the window marked 'credit'? Shall I approach a complete stranger, remind him of *Marie Antoinette* or *Around the World in Eighty Days* and ask him to lend me $1,000? I dread the inevitable brush with security and decide I am safer in bed. I must soon be packed and off, and have just enough money for the taxi fare to the airport. I won't need any money at LAX. Just check the baggage and make it to the VIP lounge for the wait till the evening plane – champagne, the English papers, a biscuit or two and then a free dinner on the plane. Who could ask for anything more? Certainly not a very important penniless person who has simply loved every moment away from sanity.

"That enfabled rock, that ship of life, that swarming million-footed, tower-masted, and sky-soaring citadel that bears the magic name of the Island of Manhattan."
THOMAS WOLFE

I am not sure if Lindbergh had flown the Atlantic by 1938, very few others seem to have done so. I went by boat, surprised that Metro-Goldwyn-Mayer should have chosen a German line. They, in their turn, were surprised at my asking for a loan of $500. After all, I was only going to make a test and my agent had assured them, when arranging a salary, that I was extremely wealthy. The advance was necessary because I needed an overcoat. But there was a good deal of change. Mother affirmed she would never see me alive again – while she was alive that was. For me, then as now, the best part of filming abroad was that someone else paid for the ticket. I managed to hold on to my first ticket to Weston-super-Mare. I wasn't filming then, of course, but had a walk-on-part-cum-understudy in *And So To Bed*.

Was I at last going to break into films? Previously I had been summarily dismissed on the grounds of disagreeing with the director and, on another occasion, because they weren't satisfied with my portrayal of a police inspector. This time, in *Marie Antoinette*, I managed to last the course. The New York office booked a seat for me to see *Babes in Arms* with Judy Garland and Mickey Rooney, presumably so I should stay awake till it was time to catch the night flight to the coast. I managed that all right. I still think it was the best evening I've spent in the theatre, except when on stage myself. I stayed awake in the moonlight and most of the next day. We came down often to refuel. The air stewardess attributed my unaccustomed alertness to terror and kept re-assuring me.

"The pilot always sees three beacons ahead," she said. "There is nothing to worry about."

Years later Deborah Kerr recalled her children's nanny's observation on making the same trip.

"I don't think I'd care to do it again, Madam – all those rocks." But then she had been on a train.

I adored the mountains and marvelled at the flashing lights. How had they managed to position them, and there were some on the plains and even in the lakes. Our last stop was Salt Lake City. Why, oh why had the modern-day Moses tarried? A few more miles and he would have been in the green and pleasant land.

"I met a Californian who would talk California – a state so blessed, he said, in climate, none ever died there a natural death, and vigilance committees had had to organize to stock graveyards and vindicate the state's humanity."

ROBERT FROST

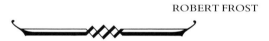

California, seen from the air, from a car, from the beaches, from the gambling boats moored outside the three-mile limit was bliss. The latter kept individual tame seals to welcome visitors. My agent warned me not to win more than my share or – like Mother – he mightn't see me again. He need not have worried. In Hollywood the one-eyed man was king – in those days the film-makers. There were privileged numbers to call the police in case of trouble. There were even armed police patrolling the lot – to stop people getting in or us getting out? I suppose the first motorways were taking shape, but our route to Culver City was along country roads and through the occasional flood. Men waited to push the car through the water and seldom charged more than a dollar.

Once my contract was signed, I talked myself out of three weeks' money before shooting began and set off for a holiday with what was left of the $500. I had been joined by a friend and settled in a flat in Westwood, then a small settlement off Sunset Boulevard. I loved the names almost as much as the places. We drove all over the area. I encouraged Llewellyn to keep turning left confident we would find our way back. California isn't the Thames Valley, but petrol was cheap and so were the motels.

I had discovered a land flowing with little hot cakes, maple syrup, corned beef hash and apple pie *à la mode*. We even managed to find Palm Springs, where the stars went – or so they said. Outside my window Simone Simon was playing tennis with Charles Boyer. Was it all a dream? I prayed not to wake up, but I already had.

The first day's filming arrived. There was a huge staircase on the set. We were in Versailles and Norma Shearer was due to descend at 9.30 a.m. precisely. No one was ever late.

"When Miss Shearer appears, everyone should courtesy," our director instructed. "You are not in the shot, but it will be good practice."

A five-piece orchestra were still dressed in modern costume, presumably they were not in the shot either. As a matter of fact, they were never filmed, just there for her pleasure and ours. They played requests.

The cameras turned, the sound came on. Miss Shearer negotiated the stairs.

"Cut and print," said Mr W. S. Van Dyke, whose latest triumph had been *The Thin Man*. No one knew less about the French Revolution or cared. He had only come on the picture the night before, when Sydney Franklin had been summarily dismissed in an effort to unsettle our star. The manoeuvre seemed to have achieved instant success.

"Surely, Mr Van Dyke, you are going for another take," Miss Shearer said. "And the word is curtsy not courtesy."

"It was all right by me, Honey," he said. "There's only one way of coming down steps. You did it just fine."

"Hollywood – where people from Iowa mistake each other for movie stars."

FRED ALLEN

After that the battle was more or less won. Miss Shearer, of course, had rushes approval, which meant an absolute power of veto on anything shot. She also had a large share of Loew's Incorporate, which Louis B. Mayer was anxious to pick up for himself. Hence the alleged harassment of his star. Once, in a moment of over-boldness, I asked her why she was a star. She had a not very attractive Canadian accent, a short, rather dumpy figure and a cast in one eye which prevented her from being photographed on occasions. "Not today," the cameraman would pronounce and all work was suspended. Of course she had married Irving Thalberg, the legendary boy genius of the lot.

"I am a star, I suppose," she told me, "because I always wanted to be one."

She had the knowledge as well as the trappings of power. She would shuffle fifty or so stills and indicate the very few that were to be printed. She walked on to the set blazing with arcs and indicated which of them was too hot for her to handle. She knew the business, but in the end surrendered her shares, married a ski-instructor, retired to Sun Valley and lived happily ever after.

We met again years later. I simply couldn't get a table at Maxim's in Paris, and scribbled a note which was delivered to her table: "It is difficult to remember these were once our subjects," and was invited to join her party.

Van Dyke treated me as if I were a novice, which of course

I was. He would ask my intentions on how I proposed to play a scene, pressed a button, never told me he was filming and hey presto it was in the can. I don't pretend I was delighted when I saw the rough cut. Everyone was there and for some reason I was terrified I would be asked my opinion and dreaded having to give it. I stumbled over the legs of the bosses and John Barrymore, and disappeared into the wastes of Culver City. Then I remembered there were supposed to be packs of wild dingos in the neighbourhood and panicked once again.

The studio had long before decided I was gay, wrote a few scenes into the film for my old friend Peter Bull, summoned him from England and afterwards cut him out of the picture. 'Anything to keep them happy' was the motto in those days. I'm not sure they kept Mr Barrymore happy. They had the French director Julien Duvivier standing by to take over from Van Dyke in an emergency. He ended up doing the second unit and mostly at night. Barrymore resented his inability to speak English, or pretended to do so. He also pretended not to be able to remember a word of the script, which he had written up on idiot boards. He also insisted on reading the wrong ones – out of sequence.

I had Greta Garbo's old dressing-room. Punctually at noon the maitre d'hôtel appeared in a tail coat and took the orders for luncheon, which was served at one. Clockwork was the rule. Once I was late arriving on the set. Van Dyke had me apologize to everyone. I climbed the gantries and shook hands with all the electricians. Then, fearing for my safety or just possibly the real ermine cloak I trailed, I was summoned below to resume my career. I rather thought I'd won that round – but I was never late again.

Once, trying to prove myself a trouper I eschewed the waiting limousine and, borrowing a messenger's bicycle, rode to my dressing-room. When he caught up with me, the owner of the bicycle was unimpressed.

"They all do it once," he sighed.

Heady days indeed. Tyrone Power and Annabella never raced each other round the lot. Only Gladys George, playing what was for her a subsidiary role, left for Pasadena Station when someone stood on her train and she was left in her petticoats.

"Get Gypsy Rose Lee," she told them.

All in all there was a good deal to report when I got back to Britain, surprised as I was to find myself there and unemployed. Uncle Louis had assured me there was more work awaiting me when I finished my stint in New York as *Oscar Wilde*.

"Meanwhile," he told me, "we'll match any offer."

I wrote cordially indicating I would be free in a fortnight, when the play closed. My agent assured me it was madness.

"I don't need to play hard to get with Mr Mayer," I told him.

A letter from the assistant to the casting director reached me some months later. If there was a suitable role for me, it indicated, I would be the first to know.

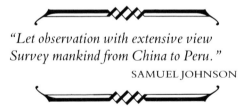

"Let observation with extensive view
Survey mankind from China to Peru."
SAMUEL JOHNSON

Left to ourselves, I doubt we would have chosen Peru, but the cruise operators suggested it was a convenient place to await embarkation for a journey down and through Magellan's Strait all the way round to Rio de Janiero. With nothing to pay except the hotel bill we decided to arrive a week earlier than necessary in Lima. Once we had inspected all the gold phalluses in the museum, there wasn't a great deal to do and the weather was gloomy. Like most places where the sea meets the mountains, smog prevails. In the library we spied a sunburned American and demanded an explanation.

"Been up the Amazon," he told us, which is why the next day we were flying to Quito. Soaring over the rain forest, we caught the occasional glimpse through the clouds.

"What's it like down there?" I asked a fellow passenger.

He told me stories of cities ruined by jungle but still containing temples filled with gold treasure – if only one could locate them.

"No kidding?" I questioned.

"Only this year an explorer returned with a golden thumb he managed to detach from a statue or what remained of a statue. It was soft gold, of course," he added.

"Soft gold?"

"He's back in there somewhere trying to find the place again. It is surprising how many crash their planes and aren't heard of again."

"I don't think I'll try anything like that," I told him. "We are aiming for the Amazon and some sun."

"In the rain forest?" he seemed surprised.

Quito was awful, just plain awful. Here vultures double as dustmen among the vast garbage tips and smells and balconies. This was, for a time, the home of Dr Eiffel. The houses had a cast-iron appearance, but were mostly the refuge of squatters. Deserted homes of once prosperous rubber and slave traders prevailed. We located our minibus, had our reservations checked for four nights in a holiday camp deep in the forest and were paddled down river (or possibly up) in a rickety canoe. There were no fellow passengers. For that matter there was no one on the banks of the Amazon. Head-hunters, crocodiles, even butterflies seemed to have disappeared. Every now and then we stopped abruptly to avoid collision with huge logs drifting towards us. It must be up river, we decided. I am not an explorer.

Not for me the deserted beach with barbed wire to climb over. I like it better where the paved bar joins the sands and the shady umbrella. Although on this occasion we didn't have to bother about shade: it poured with rain. There was some sort of canopy on the boat, but it didn't cover the luggage.

What did one expect in a rain forest? I had expected Indians fishing with cormorants, painted warriors gliding past hunting heads – not mine, of course. I yearned for the menacing beat of distant war drums. There wasn't an eagle in sight. The vultures preferred the excitement of Quito and so did I in retrospect.

Four hours later, wet, bedraggled and muddy, we reached base camp.

"Not at all what I had expected," I told the proprietor. There was no glass in the windows of the log cabin, there were no toilets, no electric light, nowhere to dry our clothes. There was not even a cupboard – but I could have sworn there was a rat hiding under the bunks.

"What did you expect?" asked the proprietor. "Television? Here we live like the Indians."

"Not at these prices, surely," I riposted unwisely.

I had made a powerful enemy. Later at supper I was convinced he had slipped me a Mickey Finn. Before it started to work we dined sparsely on Spam and surveyed our fellow sufferers. There was a couple who hunted butterflies, a Dutchman whom I thought was obviously in the drug trade and the camp cheer-leader vainly trying to raise our spirits.

"You are coming on the crocodile hunt this evening," he insisted.

"In the dark?" I queried.

"We have torches," he told us. "You can see their eyes."

I was already beginning to feel queasy, but nothing prepared me for the horror of the night as I stumbled in the mud to the lavatory every half hour with small scorpions scuttling underfoot and the ever present terror of snakes lying in wait to nip my bottom. Snatching a moment's sleep, I woke screaming, convinced something was crawling across my face. It was only my beloved wife adjusting a blanket and reassuring herself I was still breathing.

We packed at dawn. In fact, we hadn't unpacked. I sought out the proprietor, who for some reason hadn't attended the evening feast, and demanded out.

"The canoe leaves this afternoon," he told me. "If you go out, you will need an umbrella, but do not stray off the paths."

"Hostile marauders?" I queried.

"We don't like visitors disturbing the game," he replied. "Nor for that matter do they like being disturbed," he added darkly.

I lay on my bunk counting the hours to rescue. How happy I was to lie back in the canoe. The journey downstream didn't take half the time.

I was even happier that evening in a warm bath in our beautiful hotel in Lima. Funny, I hadn't thought much of it, forty-eight hours earlier. There was still the friendly cockroach, but from now on I avoided putting my foot down and crushing it. I had escaped – why shouldn't it do the same?

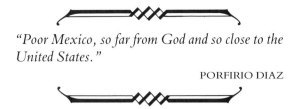

"Poor Mexico, so far from God and so close to the United States."

PORFIRIO DIAZ

The first time I saw Acapulco was on another trip with my mother-in-law. We had decided on a brief and painless exploration of Mexico avoiding all contact with Aztec ruins, which, on account of the endless flights of peculiarly narrow steps, are in my book the most uncomfortable to explore. We stayed at Cuernavaca over night and in the morning Gladys complained of having been kept awake by the continuous shunting of trains outside her window.

"Gladys," I told her sharply, "there are no trains. There is not even a railway station. We are in the depths of the country."

At breakfast I determined to obtain confirmation of my theory. The waiter sympathized with my companion.

"Trains very noisy," he admitted. "You see all the Mexican cattle come this way before they are chopped."

There were no trains to be heard in Acapulco – only the waves breaking on the beach. We stayed in a beautiful, but incomplete, empty hotel, owned, so we were told, by Mr Getty. There was fabulous air-conditioning, but for some reason it was frowned on by Gladys and all the windows had to be opened. I lived in the bathroom with cool air and a sharp attack of Mexican tummy. Then it was up and away with long walks along the shore and the occasional rifle shot in our direction from the gardens of deserted villas. Well, not quite deserted – there were the guardians. In one case at least it was a small child. Gladys set out to reason with him and possibly disarm. I fled into the sea out of range and drove sea urchins deep into my feet. Limping painfully to rejoin her I had to explain my sudden desire to paddle.

In the woods camped the, to me at any rate, intolerably poor. They lived on hammocks in disused jalopies. The children were almost naked. Gladys maintained they were all blissfully happy. They hadn't, she opined, a care in the world and only a small climb up a palm tree for luncheon.

Acapulco had yet to be exploited. I prefer exploitation and the hotel to be already *in situ*. One evening, to my relief and miles from the unfinished hotel where we were quartered, I found one that had already been built. Gladys was refused admittance as she was wearing shorts.

"Open the boutique," she told them, "and I will buy a skirt."

"No use, Madam," they replied. "The dining-room this evening is reserved for General Motors."

"The General is an old friend of mine," she countered. "He will be delighted to see me."

Gladys was seldom defeated, but on this occasion we were marched on and came to a bar, crowded with spectators awaiting the dive of death. After a time a remote figure was seen scaling the cliff and then poised to leap into the shallows below. The trick was to calculate the moment when the wave came in and there was a reasonable hope of survival. The crowd watched as at a bullfight. About once in a hundred passes the bull triumphs, but there are plenty of hopeful matadors awaiting their chance. I was reminded of the Waleska family and their high wire act over the Promenade des Anglais in Nice. The family survived – but not all the mebers in the same season. Here in Acapulco, as once in Nice, there was an opportunity to contribute conscience money when all ended safely. Once, years ago, I was watching Odett's play *Golden Boy* when the leading actor dropped fatally on the stage. Herds of hartebeest seem, at least on television, to take the attacks of lions on one of their less successful companions in their stride; for us, there is a fatal fascination with being in at the death. Is satisfaction quite the right word as we quit the cemetery?

"The rainbows in Martinique were unlike any I had ever seen, sometimes flat and straight like the side of a box. The clouds whirled in strange rushing formations. The sea glowed like burnished gunmetal under the grey sky."

QUENTIN CREWE

A day in Martinique sufficed only for snap judgements and a drive through the plantations and rain forest. The bananas wear mauve cellophane skirts and, when the bunches are cut off, the tree dies. Nature fortunately provides a stripling offspring which survives to bear fruit in its turn. I don't know what happens to the pineapples or, for that matter, the arum lilies. There are iguanas and humming birds and at the end of the trail the bus stops at the Sacré Coeur, completely recreated after its famous Parisian counterpart but without the surrounding ambience. One missed the little bar at the corner. You can't have everything, but you get a great deal in Martinique.

There was just time for a little shopping before catching the plane. A bracelet which looked like solid gold was produced for my inspection. It was of exquisite design. The price asked was US$318, at least that is what came up on the calculator.

"Make it $300," I told the girl, "and you have a deal."

"It can't be real gold," I told my wife, "or, if it is, there must be a local mine."

While I waited for her to consult the manager on my offer, I translated it into pounds sterling: give or take, £160 I calculated. Perhaps we should buy two or three. But then again there was always the question of the Customs. Still, if they are solid, as had been claimed, there must still be a reasonable profit. They were heavy. Still holding my Diner's Card, I pondered, but, when she came back, there was a dramatic change in the trading price. It semed the calculator had lied – the figure included an extra nought. If only I had paid dollars on the spot. Why am I such a fool always wanting to bargain? A quick snatch and we would have been airborne in the time it took to call out the gendarmes. Am I dishonest at heart? Yes, yes, a thousand times, yes! Look what happens if you aren't. I could even have worn the bracelet myself at a pinch – *as* a pinch, come to think of it.

"Negroes imported to the sugar islands died much faster than they were born. West Indian slave masters soon gave up trying to keep their Negroes alive long enough to breed up a new generation and instead routinely bought replacement slaves year in and year out."

RICHARD S. DUNN

Even the school run reassured in Martinique. At five, Fort de France was a moving scrum of children released from their studies being sorted and crammed by mothers on duty into waiting cars and driven off. Where? There were still plenty of sub-standard houses, but even these seemed sturdier and more habitable than the shacks of Barbados, and then too the new apartment blocks, the new housing developments impressed – and, above all, the cars. French citizens had equal status and these islanders were French. There was an emerging middle-class who could shop at one remove from the top French grocers. Printemps and Les Quatre Saisons had branches in Martinique.

The French had certainly made a go of it, though they never got around to rebuilding St Pierre after the volcano, which erupted in 1902, had overwhelmed the one-time capital which boasted an opera house, a huge cathedral and a magnificent chamber of deputies. This latter proved a deathtrap for the citizenry. Elections were about to be held when the first rumbles of the volcano were heard and the first whiff of poison gas drifted from its mouth. In an effort to contain the vote, the authorities forbade anyone to leave and erected barricades. After the holocaust only one prisoner was left alive and he in the cells under the police station. He showed his hideously scarred pelt in the circus tent until he died two years later of his injuries. His picture survived in the museum along with those of parties of white clad, helmeted and masked officials visiting the scene some days later and wearing scarves to protect themselves from the lethal fumes. There were no photographs of the citizens choking to death, but a great many drawings of men leaping into the sea clutching their throats.

In Barbados, except for the taxis catering for the visitors, the roads are for trudging. There are no branches of Marks & Spencer or Fortnum's in Bridgetown. We dined there at the Hilton Hotel. It exemplifies the reckless questing spirit of the Americas. We enquired about the goat racing (Sundays), the donkey racing (Saturdays), donkey polo and crab racing both scheduled for Wednesdays and the local coconut hat-making contest.

Donkey, let alone goat, racing would be quite unthinkable at the Sandy Lane Hotel: very up market and, one might almost say, up tight. Whereas the Hilton is situated in downtown Bridgetown (there is, alas, no uptown), the Sandy Lane lies in St James's parish. It has some of the most beautiful bedrooms and, it must be admitted, some of the most inflexible maîtres d'hôtel on the island. Here the atmosphere is rather like that on a luxury cruise liner: there are buffet nights, formal nights and international cuisine evenings.

The racing crowd who come to Barbados in the winter-time do not frequent the Sandy Lane nor even the more sporting Hilton. They are mostly to be found in rented villas along the coast. This is a time when the top trainers huddle with the racing managers and occasionally with their owners. They sit about under the trees remembering battles waged and lost, and planning others still to come. At night they patronize the Château Créole, which has a humorous mixture of lobster, flying fish and really excellent curry soup.

This is not an island growing much of its own food. Even the milk, except that served to visitors, is condensed or powdered. There is no trace of local fruit. The crops are sugar cane, yams and squash, and everything else on which the hotel guests feast is flown in from Canada, the States or Britain.

Sam Lord, who built his castle with slave labour in 1820, was a land-based pirate who apparently seldom put to sea in search of plunder but lured victims on to a convenient reef by the simple expedient of hanging lanterns on neighbouring coconut trees. What the captains expected to find under the palms or why they should assume there were smooth beaches remain a mystery, but there is no doubt the arrangement paid Lord handsomely and the castle, now a hotel and preserved as a monument to elegant tourism survives among the countless apartment blocks and bathing beaches. The ceilings are particularly fine and designed by Mr Rutter, in those days fresh from his triumphs as an interior decorator at Windsor Castle.

We drove to Crane Beach on the Atlantic side of the island. It meant a long and monotonous drive through sugar cane plantations. There can be few things more depressing than a field of sugar. One is constantly reminded of the back-breaking toil required to harvest the crop. In between the plantations, huddle the shacks of the cane workers. There is a school, a chapel, a grog shop, a bus stop and absolutely nothing else unless you count the occasional black-bellied sheep tethered to the roadside.

We stopped off the Andromeda Gardens *en route*. Mrs Iris Ballochie, whose first husband was convinced he'd never make fifty and was, alas, proved right, lived with a staff of thirty, growing exhibits for the Chelsea Flower Show along with orchids, camellias and roses, which decorated her patch and proved how much can be achieved in a garden built on a coral reef. Hurricanes, however, had a habit of catching her and her plants unawares, although she had constructed an underground shelter to which, given enough warning, they could all retreat. Recently she had found that fifteen minutes did not allow for adequate protection.

"Of course," she told me, "I know it's about the same time as you get in a nuclear war, but it isn't enough."

At Crane Beach we found the speciality of the hotel restaurant was the local fish, chub, caught only off this coast and by no means always available. There was a slightly murky Roman bath at the top of the cliffs and a rum punch at the hotel much sought after by passengers from the cruise ships which make a welcome stop *en route* for Sam Lord's Castle. On the day we visited, it was absolutely packed with cruise passengers exchanging vouchers for the regulation buffet luncheon. If, like me, you do not enjoy helping yourself at mealtimes, Barbados is not the place for you.

5
The Dark Continent

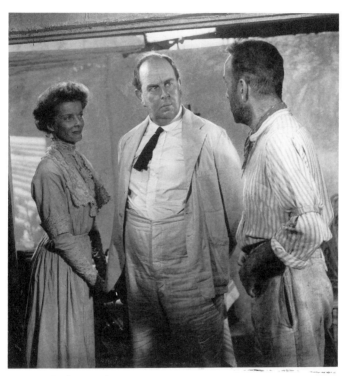

Endangered species on The African Queen *(with Katharine Hepburn and Humphrey Bogart)*

5
THE DARK CONTINENT

"Like Webster's dictionary, we're Morocco bound."
BOB HOPE AND BING CROSBY, *The Road to Morocco*

"UNTIL YOU know the Arabs really well, it's impossible to dislike them enough." My informant, a French lady who had kept a restaurant in Marrakech for twenty years, was in a bad temper brought on by staff shortages, some of her helpers having failed to turn up that morning.

Of course for tourists such as myself Marrakech has the highest credentials. It is not only where Churchill chose to paint, it also has in the main square the most fascinating djinn imaginable. You sit on a terrace with a glass of mint tea and watch everything going on at once: soothsayers, and story-tellers, letter writers and conjurors, barbers and bootblacks.

My wife and I drove down from Tangier just across from Gibraltar, having picked up a taxi from the rank and struck what seemed to me at any rate a real bargain price. We stopped at Fez, where the taxis are white steeds and perched behind the rider one loses onself in the largest *souk* in Africa. The Arabs struck me as particularly relaxed. They were happy to sit for idle hours to sell the occasional door hinge. The hotel in Fez is a palace and here I blundered, inviting the gentleman in a gorgeous uniform to summon our driver.

"I am," he told me, "the personal equerry of the King of Libya." Point taken and never forgotten.

Fez seemed a long way from the Mamounia Hotel in Marrakech, where there was no problem in identifying the hall porter. Further along the sand dunes, a good deal further over the Atlas mountains is the oasis of Taroudant. Here we met up with the most eminent theatre critic of his day (and a good time after), Kenneth Tynan. He wasn't staying, as we were, at the Golden Gazelle as we had secured the last bungalow, but he came to lunch round the pool and to stare into its opaque depths. His was the perpetual quest for hashish, which he thought might cure his emphysema, which was by that time chronic. Not particularly efficient in mime – but then what theatre critic is? – he was always signalling his hope of being supplied to anyone he came across on our picnics. His antics always drew a small crowd of local children or a wine waiter who attended us in a restaurant. It was useless for the maître d'hôtel to point out that the handling of drugs carried a severe penalty. On picnics, with no maître d'hôtel to intervene, an occasional child would scamper off into the bushes and return with a half-smoked packet of Camel cigarettes. Ken would light up with the composure of a man lighting a cigar he knows to contain a cracker and is anxious not to spoil the enjoyment of the others. Much to my relief, he was always to be disappointed. Travelling would not be half so much fun if the element of anxiety was entirely removed, but I didn't really enjoy the prospect of being stoned to death or far more probably to lose the profitable account paid me by British Airways as their spokesperson.

Ken urged that we should hire a car and visit the valley of the blue Bedouins. I don't know what I expected, although I was pretty sure by this time what it was he expected to find there. There is no such thing as a blue Arab – it is just that the clothing they wear is dyed conservatively. So we were both disappointed. Still I shall never forget Tynan going through the gestures of a man lighting up, puffing deeply and then suddenly lying down on his back and closing his eyes in feigned ecstasy. Fellow diners thought he had died. Perhaps I am a shade harsh about Ken. He wasn't exactly Marcel Marceau, but then the latter never wrote as Ken once did, "The cast is dressed to kill and what it is dressed to kill is the play."

I never had much time for the late Sir Peter Scott. His pursuit of pink-footed geese on pony back in Iceland struck me as an unhelpful activity. These days they ring prisoners on remand, so I suppose in his time he was something of an innovator. People, including myself, pleaded for the goslings separated from their families. He never, I think, bothered to answer his correspondents and I suppose he died knowing more about his quarry than I did. It was the same in Zimbabwe whither I was dispatched by the travel promotion department of the local tourist board to drum up trade. My efforts, alas, met with little success. By the time I had completed my enquiries, tourists were inopportunely massacred on the road from Bulawayo to Victoria Falls. A friend or rather an acquaintance of mine was paid by some obscure American do-gooder to anesthetize leopards, fit them with radio transmitters and discover if they were breaking bounds in the dusk. The trouble for him was that it took time for the effect of the anesthetic to wear off and, while his victims slept, he was obliged to watch over them lest they should be devoured by other carnivores. Invited to share his vigil, I thankfully refused. What if the beast should wake unexpectedly and, still disoriented by the drug, savage me?

I never understood elephants or tigers, or they me for that matter. If anything qualifies as an endangered species it must surely be mankind. It is extraordinary how the phrase caught on. I am not your man when it comes to bouncing around game reserves trying to spot the ever elusive bongo. Apart from anything else, I usually fail to do so.

"There," the guide urges as we survey the desolate terrain

from the stalled jeep, "surely you glimpsed him just disappearing into the thicket?"

"By Jove, yes," I reply. "How fortunate we are."

All the time I wonder if the jeep will restart.

"I am a little bit closer to this herd of elephant than I would wish," he told me on another occasion. "I think it would be wiser if you ignored them. Cameras away."

In my bungalow some hours later I found a list of the animals and birds we were supposed to have sighted. Gratefully I ticked off "elephant". If I'd been a cheat I would have added "bongo". When they flooded the valley for the Kariba dam, someone left a small island right in the middle. On their annual exodus the game swim out to it, find they can't proceed any further and often drown in the attempt to complete their journey. They make a welcome feast for the crocodiles. I should be grateful, I suppose, that the Duke of Edinburgh's worries are not mine – nor mine his for that matter.

Doctor Livingstone did well to discover the Victoria Falls. Once they ran luxury trains to them from Cape Town with a few nights at the beautiful hotel nearby. A stroll through the garden and you were on the brink, lashed by spray and eaten by mosquitoes. There was not a tiger in sight. There was even a casino down the road, but something misfired in a ground-to-air missile shot from the other side of the border – or else they mistook the brightly lit establishment for a hostile plane – and the punters perished along with the premises.

There were plans to rebuild it, of course. There are always plans to rebuild in Africa. Perhaps they have even managed to rebuild the tourist trade – I certainly hope so. It will do much to alleviate the anxieties of the wildlife which arrives in the evening dutifully to lick the salt, drink at the waterholes and anxiously count their endangered guests browsing and sluicing in the dining-room.

6
Eastern Mysteries

Controlling myself when faced with non-violence

6
EASTERN
MYSTERIES

"The Japanese have perfected good manners and made them indistinguishable from rudeness."

PAUL THEROUX

I ARRIVED IN Tokyo via Nakoda and Yokohama still haunted by a model of a Tsarist prisoner chained to a wheelbarrow which I had glimpsed in Irkutsk. It seemed that those who offended authority were similarly treated on arrival and spent the rest of their brief lives permanently attached to the handle. I thought in those days it was the cruellest fate of which I would ever be made aware. Worse was to follow, but not, of course, in the capital of Japan, where I felt I had disturbed a colony of ants. From the window of the Hilton I watched elegant ladies exchanging gift-wrapped parcels. I enquired about the contents.

"Sugar," I was told.

I explored the department stores, where enormous and beautiful fish swam happily in their glass tanks, and walked up the Ginza to play the pin tables. I found out what the Japanese do with surplus ball bearings – pachinko machines. I was very much one of a crowd and the only one not in a hurry.

I took the bullet train to Kyoto and inspected the temples, joining a group led everywhere by a guide carrying aloft a pink flag. It seemed important at the time not to lose sight of his tiny banner. I paid my respects to a small dog who looked as if he might have been carved by Landseer except that I had never heard of him sculpting anything.

As usual, not speaking the language, I confined my acquaintanceship to Americans in the hotel bar. Most of them seemed to be gay and were living Japanese-style with Monsieur Butterflies. I was asked to dinner with one or two, took my shoes off outside the front door and usually fell into a small pit around the dining-room table.

One evening I was entertained geisha style. Saki was poured for me into miniature glasses by perpetually smiling ladies, who occasionally popped raw fish into my mouth. Afterwards one or two of the ladies danced – but not with us. I realized with relief that we were not expected to make advances. How, I wondered, would it have been possible or even seemly to undress a geisha?

I visited a kabuki theatre, where performances started early in the afternoon. I told myself it would be easy to slip away for dinner, but found myself happily stuck there until after midnight, fascinated by the wailing and the mime of elderly men dressed as medieval princesses.

There didn't seem to be any cherry blossom to observe. Only the base of Mount Fuji was visible – the top was perpetually wreathed in cloud. There were, however, enormous Buddhas, in front of whom the faithful juggled with bundles of chopsticks to discover what lay in wait for them. I tried my luck and donated my small change to the resident soothsayer. Naturally it was not enough, so I increased the stake.

"You are destined to take a long journey," I was told.

So I flew home. I was tired of being mistaken for Babe Ruth and on one occasion Laird Creegar.

"He is dead," I told them brutally, "gone to join his ancestors."

"The logistics of organizing tourism in China are among the most complex in the world . . . Scheduled itineraries are frequently subject to unpredictable changes . . . It would be better to visit China sooner rather than later, as no doubt the pollutant effects of tourism will tarnish the freshness and sense of uniqueness which makes travel to China such a pleasurable and rewarding experience."

ELIZABETH MORRELL

"Paddle," urged Miss Faithful.

"It's shingle," I told her.

"I brought you here to enjoy yourself and enjoy yourself you shall."

Our governess was something of a disciplinarian. She didn't last. If there was one thing my sister and I were expert at, it was getting rid of these creatures.

Miss Faithful's attitude prevailed in China. No one has ever asked me to make a picture there, so, for once, I was paying for myself and my youngest child. The tour started at the Mandarin Hotel in Hong Kong. I have always been fond of that joint – even when I did three weeks there in cabaret. It was not an unqualified success. I attracted only a small audience – mostly Japanese, who didn't speak my language. During my turn I ate caviar and drank champagne, following the rule of the British abroad: eat out of tins properly labelled and never drink the water.

The Japanese seldom laughed and when the English-speaking lot predominated, I went on far too long and gave them excerpts from Wilde, continuing until I had finished the bottle. I still remember the jade market, where it is sold sight unseen. The piece of rock you acquire may or may not contain a sizeable chunk. You have, after the purchase, to break it open with a hammer. If you are not an expert, you shatter the contents. They sell it in a mock auction and the Chinese buy in silence, clutching hands. A squeeze and the transaction is completed. But there was no time for the jade market on this visit. We were destined for the mainland.

We were introduced to our fellow explorers at a cocktail party and a complimentary feast. We were warned not to expect the same luxury on our journey, so we were sent to bed and prepared for an early flight.

On the plane, breakfast was an orange, a bag of mixed toffees and a toothpick.

Our first destination was Suzhou, the flower city beloved by gardeners and artists. My son and I woke early in our bedroom, ordered an elaborate breakfast of toast, eggs, bacon, fresh orange juice and coffee. All that arrived after a long delay was the inevitable thermos flask of tepid water and some raw tea leaves. Dressing hastily, we climbed into the minibus.

The star of our little group was an American lady of well over eighty, who was accompanied by her grandchildren. The teenagers explained to our tour master that grandmother couldn't do stairs. Of course she did; she had to. We never seemed to eat at a restaurant that wasn't on the second floor. Temples were all stairs – but she did have to consent sometimes to wait in the car park. Miss Faithful would have loved her. Her enthusiasm and enjoyment were unbounded. Her special love was for prehistoric sites. She claimed to have visited most of the extant jungle ruins, gardens in Babylon and she even enthused about Stonehenge. She was longing to see the Great Wall, which was why she had kidnapped her brood to China. They were a good deal less enthusiastic – so indeed was my own son.

"Not another jade Buddha, surely?" they expostulated. "Once you've seen one, you've seen them all – or at least you hope you have."

It was the same with the paddy fields and the water buffalo

and, of course, the bicycles.

There is a small park on the esplanade at Shanghai and near by it a notice still reads, "No dogs or Chinese permitted" to remind us of our manners in these parts.

The food was disappointing. If you are on a package holiday in China, you get a package breakfast, soup and fish – sometimes together, sometimes apart. We never knew what was coming next as one tureen followed another. I craved marmalade and set out to buy some. You can buy television sets in most of the shops, but jams elude. I brought back a bottle of hot pickles and explained my problem to a local who instantly disappeared with my foreign currency to the hotel kitchen returning with the genuine Oxford variety.

"Plenty more where that came from," he told me. "All you have to do is find the head cook."

Of course the trouble is most of the head cooks have left China to set up small restaurants in Lowestoft.

There really was no point in a tiresome journey to Xian to see the terracotta warriors. When I got home they were being exhibited in Selfridge's.

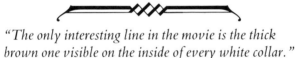

"The only interesting line in the movie is the thick brown one visible on the inside of every white collar."

JOHN SIMON

Mr Birla, while appreciating the need to photograph his kitchen garden for the filming of scenes concerning Gandhi, had given instructions that the cast should be confined to the garage and not allowed in the house. The assassination, of course, had actually taken place on the front lawn, but Mr Birla had decided that the cabbage patch made a more convenient shrine and place of pilgrimage. For the first time I entertained grave doubts about the Mahatma. How had he brought himself to accept the hospitality of one who held the acting profession in such low regard?

Gandhi in the film *Nine Hours to Rama* was played by an amateur impresario who had assured the producers that just to portray his hero was recompense enough. He was not universally popular and suffered from an exceedingly weak bladder, which frequently obliged him to absent himself just at the moment the cameras were ready to turn – which was a fairly rare occasion in any case.

His Indian colleagues were wont to sit around taunting him with the imaginary sums they were themselves receiving for their services.

"I am buying, Mr Morley, a hotel in Kensington Gardens and have been recommended Waring & Gillows to furnish? Can you tell me if they are a truly reliable firm?"

In the end he cracked and asked me to recommend a reliable actors' agent.

"Too late," I told him, rather heartlessly perhaps.

Once, at a Delhi dinner party at ambassadorial level, I incautiously remarked I was not certain that I personally would be born again – even as a Christian.

"You must meet Sister Hannah before you leave," I was advised. "I will arrange an audience."

Sister Hannah subsequently agreed to see me at three o'clock one morning. It seeemed a strange hour. I was not prepared for the small bungalow on a new estate in which the sorceress was temporarily domiciled. I had been informed that no politician ever took an important decision without first obtaining her opinion. Also, of course, she had been the confidante of "Mickey Mouse", the name by which Gandhi's own kitchen cabinet always referred to him.

"Let me see your hands," she demanded from the camp bed on which she reclined. "I'm afraid you are a gambler," she remarked as I willingly complied. I have always been rather proud of my hands.

She explained that her present phase of meditation had made her extremely allergic to punters. She allowed me to remain seated – near an open window. The only other remarks she made to me directly were that I should be more careful when I drove a car (how true) and that I should never question my purpose in life as, in my case, it was neither necessary nor desirable. After that the talk was largely political and fairly malicious.

Sister Hannah occasionally reminisced, recalling an occasion when, in prison with "Mickey", he had refused a saline injection. The prison doctor, in the absence of volunteers, had prepared the syringe and leant over the patient preparing to administer the injection, whereupon Gandhi spoke to him, but so quietly that no one else heard what he said.

"I can only tell you," remarked Sister Hannah, "that the back of the physician's neck turned a curious purple, he abandoned the attempt and left Delhi the next morning never to return."

"What do you suppose he said?" I asked.

"Of course we questioned him later, but the Mahatma purported not to remember . He was in a very weak state you must understand. Everyone thought he was dying."

But he lived on to perish among the rose beds. We drove back to Delhi in an almost impenetrable fog, which persisted the next morning, when I resumed my role and found that the coloured contact lenses I had been allocated were frozen solid in their case. I sat on the coffin in the great funeral procession with my blue eyes tightly shut while marigolds were flung at the bier by the cast crowd of extra mourners. Of course I shouldn't really have been sitting on the coffin, but that was a mistake by the director.

It was my mistake to go to the races later in the day. I didn't dare tell the locals what I had been doing that morning but news travels fast in Delhi.

"Tell me, Mr Morley, you were actually seated on top of

the Mahatma?" they questioned in disbelief.

I prefer to remember a subsequent incident when an enraged mob invaded the stewards' enclosure to protest at the state of the betting where the favourite had rapidly advanced from the initial price of odds on. The steward, versed in the situation, immediately dispatched another jockey, in a car, to the starting post only to have it narrowly avoid a collision with the horses who had already begun the race. In any case, the favourite won and the jockey was loudly booed as he entered the winning enclosure. Some punters are never satisfied.

On the whole I enjoyed my first visit to India. It is always easier when someone else is paying. Subsequently I treated myself to a visit to Bombay and Goa.

Over dinner in Bombay I chided Mr Patel over the prices charged at the Taj Mahal hotel, which had been built back to front contrary to the architect's instructions.

"Give me complimentary seats for any production in which you are appearing and I will see to your account," he said.

"Snap," I told him.

He only once subsequently availed himself of my offer. He brought a party of eight to the Savoy Theatre and left after the first interval. My hotel bill had obviously been larger than he had anticipated.

Goa was a disaster. We went in a taxi without air-conditioning and with a driver who was unsure of the route. After twenty hours we arrived and found the hotel full, and a gala party in progress. We drank champagne and our party of four was fully accommodated in a hostel bedroom meant for the staff. The next day I sat around being photographed with small Indian children perched on my lap until the management conceded I was worthy of better accommodation and I was able to dislodge the small fry and spend my time in the swimming-pool.

Sitting among the marigolds – it was the director's fault.

"On the whole, Turks are, and always have been sharp dressers . . . Hats in politics go back much further (than the Hat Law of 1925). As far back as the 1460s Mehmet the Conqueror was enacting a hat law governing the colours of turbans that could be worn at court: green for vezirs, red for chamberlains, white for muftis, red, yellow or black for everyone else except infidels, who weren't allowed a turban at all. Mehmet followed this up with a shoe ordinance."

CADOGAN GUIDE TO TURKEY

As far as I am concerned, things are never entirely normal in Turkey. Once, for example, I found myself driving round and round Izmir in an open carriage with the head of a BBC mission to the radio and television exhibition which was taking place in that city and where the Corporation had rented a small stand, on which my companion had sat dressed in pyjamas ("You have to observe the customs of the country," he insisted). In the cab he cast me as Pooh Bah in *The Mikado* and sang the songs over and over as we drove round and round. He had also, he assured me, engaged the massed bands of the Brigade of Guards to appear on subsequent evenings. It was going to be a tight squeeze. One performance of *The Mikado* would be enough – you don't want to spoil them. How often the Guards were to perform hadn't apparently been decided. What had been decided was that he was to be flown to Istanbul in the morning for medical assessment. It was my task to sit with him for the night lest he should decide on another sortie to the exhibition, from which he had been banned following a persistent attempt on his part to wrestle the Mayor.

"Do you understand about Turkish wrestling?" he asked me. "You catch hold of the pyjama cord and go for the balls.

Of course the Mayor wasn't wearing his pyjamas, so naturally I lost. But I shall demand a rematch. Representing the Beeb, as I do, one must be prepared to show the flag. That is why I have ordered a Rolls Royce. It is due to be delivered in the morning."

But in the morning they bore him aloft and I never did find out what happened to him.

The very afternoon I arrived in Istanbul to make *Topkapi* I was dressed as an English housewife interviewing a prospective candidate for cook-housekeeper. The words were my own, it was an impromptu performance, but the dress was loaned me by a keen amateur group who had convinced me to join them as they competed for the annual shield. They assured me they always won, just as they insisted I should join the club on Princess Island for luncheon and a swim. I had taken the morning ferry, and although I knew the club premises were private, feigned ignorance and was admitted. With my help the drama prize that year went elsewhere. You can't win them all.

Topkapi seemed to demand endless journeys in an open car with Melina Mercouri, Maximilian Schell and Peter Ustinov. Maximilian gave impromptu Schubert recitals in the evenings, and Peter and I competed to amuse Melina. When asked afterwards for her reactions, she confided that she seldom understood a word either of us was saying, but that she made a point of laughing heartily as soon as we stopped talking, which wasn't often enough.

We were also filmed for hours in the stadium, watching genuine wrestlers oiled all over, topless and trying for the traditional holds. There were bears who for lira walked over the customers, massaging their backs in the dust. Should I, I wondered, import one to Britain and exhibit a notice advertising "Bear Massages" and wait for the unwary to point out the I had misspelt my wares?

I even lured my agent to visit. He arrived with the address of a gentleman who was supposed to run an exceptionally smart brothel. It turned out to be a carpet shop. There was certainly no sign of further Turkish delights.

"Come on," I begged him. "Your informant was mis-informed. He no doubt has never laid anything but a rug."

We were not to escape so easily. My agent remarked that he was not in a buying mood. All he could offer was a tenth of the price demanded. His bid was successful and the patchwork thrust into his arms. In vain he protested that he hadn't been serious and dropped it on the floor. We fled together with the taunt of "perfidious Albion" ringing in our ears.

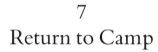

7
Return to Camp

Meanwhile, back home . . .

7
RETURN
TO CAMP

"I have seen the Mississippi. That is muddy water. I have seen the St Lawrence. That is crystal water. But the Thames is liquid history."

JOHN BURNS

IT WAS ADVERTISED in the personal columns of *The Times* and it wasn't all that easy to find. You went through the village of Wargrave, up a hill and then along a straight road. Suddenly, rounding a corner, there it was. The house had been condemned, but was being resuscitated by the local builder, who was kneeling in the passage affixing tiles. I took £50 off the asking price and he rose silently and shook my hand. Houses were cheap in those days, particularly in that neck of the woods, and the neck of a wood was where it stood. There were nine acres which I subsequently bought from the timber merchant who had finished chopping down the oak. He had left a sapling, which had taken root in the field by the front of the cottage.

"I think we should get rid of this if you want a front lawn," we were told by the landscape gardener.

"Leave it," advised my father-in-law. "You might need a bit of shade."

In fifty years the plane tree has grown to a formidable height. Now it is almost too much of a good thing.

Wargrave, down the road, is classed as a riverside village. It still holds the Thames record for the largest chub, caught there in 1897. It weighed 113 ounces. The access to the river, however, is now somewhat limited unless you live on the bank. Riparian rights dominate. Once I ran my punt aground and a madman flew across his lawn.

"You can't stop here," he shouted.

"Only for a fortnight," I told him. "My holiday," I explained. "I would be grateful for the use of your bathroom – at stated hours, naturally."

He retreated and emerged with a rifle, and the craft, sensing the crisis, disengaged and drifted on.

We used to bathe in the river. Strict protocol existed at the adjacent yacht club. Once, in one of the darkest hours of Dunkirk, an old gentleman quit the premises in his dinghy. He was halted by another man running along the back with a megaphone.

"Commodore," he was hailed. "are you going ashore? Shall I haul down your pennant?"

The garage proprietor had a reputation for meanness. Every week when the fish and chip van appeared it was his habit to purchase only enough for himself. His family was told that the supply was exhausted or the quality not up to scratch. A posse was formed. Torch-bearers invited his wife to accompany them. He was brusquely illuminated munching his solitary meal on the river bank. The practice ceased, but so did the marriage.

During the war our electrician doubled as a special constable. He was a firm friend, who once alerted me when danger threatened.

"Special Branch were down yesterday," he told me, "enquiring about you."

"Do they think I'm a spy?"

"Possibly. You were reported as spreading alarm and

despondency," he quoted from his notebook. "You were heard to say, 'I don't mind having my back against a wall, that is if I can find one left standing.' I should be a bit more careful if I were you," he told me.

"What could happen?" I asked. "Prison?"

"They're more likely to call you up," he opined.

Mine was an inglorious war. Perhaps if I had known the full horror I might have waived my status in a reserved occupation and tried harder to assist. But I resented an earlier interview with a Reading recruiter who, after indicating my medical category, refused further elucidation as to why I was classed so low.

"It simply means what it says," he informed me, "you are not A-1."

He showed me a list of how I could best be employed in the war effort. I opted first to be trained as a cook, an application he ruled out, and then I told him I might prefer a small office in Reading, where I could direct others to be sent hither and thither.

"I shall put you down for Air Force, clerk, special duties," he said.

"Entailing what?" I pressed on unwisely.

"Staying in the control room until it is blown to pieces," he rejoined smugly.

My wife was waiting to drive me home with the last of the petrol.

"I am not only seriously ill," I told her, "but it also seems I am expendable."

As it happened, the petrol gauge was faulty, but even before we stopped I felt stranded.

"Nothing unites the English like war."

HUGH MILLS

Although I had fled to Wargrave from a penthouse on the top of Arlington House as the bombs began to fall on the capital, I was up in London most evenings playing at the Savoy in *The Man Who Came To Dinner*. I was terrified that a near explosion might cause me to be the first to scream and, I suppose, duck. The audiences were imperturbable. In the bowels of the Savoy they felt secure and even stayed on after the performance if a raid persisted. We attempted to entertain with impromptu efforts, but never for long. The audience soon sought sanctuary in the streets, escaping from amateur conjurors and actors reciting "If". When we had emptied the auditorium, we were free to go home ourselves. With London burning there was a further hazard: those with carrier bags were liable to be stopped and searched for contraband soap. Sooner and usually later I reached Paddington Station and caught the train to Wargrave and bicycled puffing up the hill to the cottage.

I remember the poster of another conflict with the child on his father's knee. "What did you do in the Great War, Daddy?" Luckily, mine never asked. All I could have shown them were press cuttings. Volumes of them stacked in the Colt house, which I built at the bottom of the garden – or rather Mr Colt did. I think even Quentin Crisp would be proud of its perpetual cigar ash, its uneasy piles of unanswered mail, the exhausted disposable lighters, the pens dry of ink and the discarded junk mail that have accumulated in my fifty years' residence. Every now and then I look through the French windows across the lawn and marvel at how little has changed during that time except perhaps whereas people once walked along the road or bicycled they now run and motor.

I occasionally attend meetings at the village hall or the school. The latter, I admit, is unrecognizable from when I first came here. The first infants' school was opened on Crazies Hill in July 1861 and was financed by subscriptions.

It stood for over a hundred years before it was replaced. The parents are still subscribing. Now, instead of trudging along my road, the children all arrive in cars at spanking new premises and a strictly unspanking headmaster. The catchment area has been extended and it is easier to go on from there to Eton. The parents are resourceful and endlessly improving the property, once the prerequisite of private schoolmasters, tirelessly exhorting the parents to provide gymnasiums and swimming-pools. I recently attended a function where champagne flowed and I unveiled a new classroom and a small plaque on the wall which bore the date of the ceremony and, to my unconcealed delight, my own name. In truth I have done little to help except to live longer than most. There I met one of the parents who was an unashamed property developer.

"It's an easy life," he told me. "Once every two or so years I search out a cottage in a large field remote from neighbours, pull it down and build a decent house."

I don't think there are any such properties left around here. I remember my gardener who, when called up as a fireman in the war, took a liking to the bright lights, lost all interest in the state of the rhododendron and finally sold his small semi-detached at a huge profit and moved to Brixton. They've all gone now – the handymen, the farm hands, the gardeners, the bricklayers – even the postmistress who drowned herself in her own well. The rural population with one up and one down and an outside lavatory is no more. Now we have fitted bathrooms and, in a settlement that sports advertisements on the telephone post for a Neighbourhood Watch Committee, there is, it seems, only one last resident housebreaker. He too will soon disappear, I suppose.

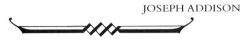

"When men are easy in their circumstances, they are naturally enemies to innovations".

JOSEPH ADDISON

The village hall is reserved for elderly residents banded together as an association to try and prevent anything happening. My neighbour is an enchanting farmer's wife from Iran and on her behalf I appeared briefly and unsuccessfully among them to plead on the suitability of a golf course to replace dilapidated farm buildings. These are, after all, difficult times for farmers and the Government, tired of subsidies, urged them to diversify. What about golf courses, eventing centres, small airstrips for amateur gliders? When the farmers try, of course, the outraged residents object because of the narrowness of the roads or the nuisance to be caused by hot-air balloons. If there is one thing the residents cannot abide, it is a housing estate. They've got their home and demand that no one else should have one.

The most vociferous among the protestors, the most anti-change, are the newcomers. They weren't here when the Vikings plundered the Wargrave settlement in their raids along the Thames valley in the twelfth century. They weren't even here in the eighteenth century, when the youthful Lord Barrymore built what was then the most modern theatre in England in the village. It held as many as 750 people and not only did he build the theatre but also cottages for the artistes who arrived from London. But then there have always been dissenters. The theatre was burned to the ground within six years under suspicious circumstances. Some time later the village church was also burned down by suffragettes angered by the vicar's refusal to remove the word "obey" from the marriage service. I was not here then either, of course, but I have been here a long time.

Envoi

"The world, which took six days to make, is like to take six thousand to make out."

SIR THOMAS BROWNE

ACCORDING TO MY pocket calculator, I've had, in eighty-one years travelling the world, 29,565 days – and that is not counting leap years, which would make the calculation too difficult for me. I have still not made it out.

If, as I have always thought, life is a party, I should be leaving quite soon. Mustn't outstay my welcome. On the whole I've enjoyed it all tremendously – not quite all, but never mind. I would like to thank my host for having asked me, but where has he gone, and who is he exactly? Perhaps, if I knew why I'd been invited, it might give me a clue. No matter, I'll just collect my shroud and be off. Where to exactly? Is there another party just up the road? This one has been very seductive, but has Mother Earth fallen in love with me as I have with her? Could I have done more to attract her?

Have I really been all around the world in any real sense? Usually I just scratched the surface where pleasure lies not too deeply buried. Often have I avoided the cathedral for the casino, the picture gallery for the picture palace. Now I am content to watch it go by on television and am grateful not to have to stir from my armchair to join it. I once wrote that I would like to die with the taste of gin and tonic on my lips, but I have changed my mind. I would prefer death to come when my eyes are wide open, gazing at the television on which there is a picture of a giant sloth swimming unconcernedly in the delta of the Amazon. The slaves who built the Colossus at Rhodes have evolved into the cameramen who scale impossible heights and plumb impossible depths to bring the world to me. It has all been very enjoyable – the world.